BASICS OF PHARMACOLOGY

MR. VISHESH KUMAR MAURYA

MS. AFSHA KHAN

DR. VIKAS SAXENA

Made with ♥ on the Notion Press Platform
www.notionpress.com

This book is dedicated to the visionaries, researchers, educators, and healthcare professionals who have dedicated their lives to the field of pharmacology—a discipline that stands at the intersection of science and medicine, shaping the future of healthcare with every discovery and innovation.

To the pioneering scientists and researchers, whose relentless curiosity and dedication to uncovering the mysteries of drug action have led to groundbreaking therapies. Your tireless efforts in laboratories, clinical trials, and academic discussions have paved the way for life-saving medications, transforming the way we understand and treat diseases.

To the educators and mentors, who inspire and guide the next generation of pharmacologists with wisdom and passion. Your commitment to teaching, your ability to ignite curiosity, and your unwavering belief in the power of knowledge have helped shape countless students into skilled professionals.

To the students of pharmacology, whose thirst for knowledge and determination to make a difference will define the future of medicine. May this book serve as a stepping stone in your journey, helping you navigate the complexities of drug interactions, mechanisms, and therapeutic applications.

To the clinicians and healthcare providers, who translate pharmacological principles into life-saving treatments, ensuring the safe and effective use of medications for patients around the world. Your dedication to patient care and evidence-based medicine is the heart of pharmacology in practice.

To the pharmaceutical industry professionals and regulatory bodies, who work tirelessly to bring new drugs to market, ensuring their safety, efficacy, and accessibility. Your efforts behind the scenes make it possible for millions to have access to essential medications.

And most importantly, to the patients, whose struggles and triumphs remind us of the profound impact of pharmacology on human life. Your resilience is the driving force behind every breakthrough, and your well-being remains the ultimate goal of this field.

May this book serve as a beacon of knowledge, inspiration, and progress, contributing to the ever-evolving field of pharmacology and its mission to improve lives across the globe.

Mr. Vishesh Kumar Maurya

Ms. Afsha Khan

Dr. Vikas Saxena

Contents

Foreword

Pharmacology, the science of drugs and their interactions with living systems, is an ever-evolving field that plays a crucial role in modern medicine. From the development of life-saving antibiotics to the cutting-edge advancements in personalized medicine, pharmacology has shaped the way we understand and treat diseases. This book is a testament to the progress, challenges, and future possibilities within this dynamic discipline.

In today's rapidly advancing world, the study of pharmacology is more important than ever. With the emergence of novel drug therapies, increasing concerns about antimicrobial resistance, the rise of biotechnology, and the integration of artificial intelligence in drug discovery, pharmacology continues to push the boundaries of medical science. The need for well-informed professionals who can navigate the complexities of drug action, safety, and therapeutic application is paramount.

This book is designed to serve as a comprehensive guide for students, educators, researchers, and healthcare practitioners. It provides a deep understanding of pharmacokinetics, pharmacodynamics, drug classifications, mechanisms of action, and clinical applications, along with discussions on recent innovations and ethical considerations in drug development. The content is structured to offer a balance between fundamental principles and advanced concepts, making it a valuable resource for both beginners and seasoned professionals.

One of the defining strengths of this book is its emphasis on evidence-based practice and real-world applications. Pharmacology is not just about understanding how drugs work at the molecular level; it is about applying that knowledge to improve patient outcomes. Through case studies, clinical correlations, and discussions on emerging drug therapies, this book connects theoretical knowledge with practical implications, ensuring that readers develop a holistic understanding of the subject.

Furthermore, this book highlights the multidisciplinary nature of pharmacology, demonstrating its intersection with physiology, biochemistry, pathology, and even artificial intelligence and nanotechnology in drug delivery. The integration of these diverse fields underscores the importance of collaboration in medical research and healthcare, reminding us that pharmacology is not an isolated discipline but a cornerstone of therapeutic advancements.

As we move forward into an era of precision medicine, pharmacogenomics, and AI-driven drug discovery, it is crucial to equip students and professionals with the necessary knowledge and critical thinking skills to adapt and innovate. This book serves as both a foundation and a springboard for those who wish to explore the depths of pharmacology and contribute to its future.

I commend the authors for their dedication to this work and for creating a resource that is both comprehensive and accessible. Whether you are a student beginning your journey in pharmacology, a researcher seeking deeper insights, or a healthcare provider looking to enhance patient care, this book will be an invaluable companion in your pursuit of knowledge.

With great enthusiasm, I invite you to delve into the pages ahead, explore the fascinating world of pharmacology, and become part of a field that continuously shapes the future of medicine.

Mr. Vishesh Kumar Maurya

Ms. Afsha Khan

Dr. Vikas Saxena

Preface

Pharmacology is a cornerstone of modern medicine, bridging the gap between scientific research and clinical practice. It is the foundation upon which we understand how drugs interact with biological systems, providing insights into their mechanisms, therapeutic applications, potential side effects, and safety profiles. The study of pharmacology is not only essential for medical professionals but also for researchers, pharmacists, and students who aspire to contribute to the advancement of healthcare.

This book has been written with the aim of offering a comprehensive yet accessible resource on pharmacology, catering to both students and professionals in the field. Recognizing the dynamic nature of this discipline, we have structured the content to cover fundamental concepts, clinical applications, and recent advancements in drug discovery and development.

Objectives of This Book

The primary objective of this book is to provide a solid foundation in pharmacology, ensuring that readers gain a deep understanding of:

Pharmacokinetics and Pharmacodynamics – The principles governing drug absorption, distribution, metabolism, and excretion, as well as drug-receptor interactions and mechanisms of action.

Drug Classifications and Therapeutic Applications – A systematic overview of various drug classes, their indications, and their effects on different physiological systems.

Clinical Correlations – Practical applications of pharmacology in clinical settings, highlighting drug interactions, adverse effects, and patient-centered care.

Recent Innovations in Pharmacology – Emerging trends such as pharmacogenomics, biologics, nanomedicine, and artificial intelligence in drug discovery.

Who Should Read This Book?

This book is designed to serve a diverse audience:

Undergraduate and postgraduate students of pharmacy, medicine, nursing, and life sciences seeking a structured and detailed understanding of pharmacology.

Researchers and academicians who wish to explore the latest advancements in drug research and development.

Healthcare professionals including physicians, pharmacists, and nurses who need a reference guide for clinical pharmacology.

Unique Features of This Book

To enhance learning and retention, this book incorporates the following features:

Clear and concise explanations with diagrams, tables, and flowcharts for easy understanding.

Clinical case studies to illustrate real-world applications of pharmacological principles.

Key takeaways and summary sections at the end of each chapter for quick revision.

Discussion of recent research and future directions in drug discovery and precision medicine.

Mr. Vishesh Kumar Maurya

Ms. Afsha Khan

Dr. Vikas Saxena

Acknowledgements

The completion of this book on Pharmacology has been a journey of dedication, research, and collaboration. It would not have been possible without the support, guidance, and encouragement of numerous individuals and institutions. We take this opportunity to express our deepest gratitude to everyone who has contributed to making this work a reality.

Academic and Research Contributors

First and foremost, we extend our heartfelt gratitude to our mentors and professors, whose invaluable guidance and expertise in pharmacology have played a pivotal role in shaping our understanding of this subject. Their dedication to education and research has inspired us to delve deeper into the complexities of drug interactions, therapeutic applications, and the ever-evolving landscape of pharmacology.

A special thanks to our colleagues and fellow researchers, whose insightful discussions, critical reviews, and shared knowledge have enriched the content of this book. Their contributions in refining key concepts, verifying data, and providing constructive feedback have ensured the accuracy and relevance of the material presented.

Support from Institutions and Organizations

We are deeply appreciative of the support received from universities, research institutions, and pharmaceutical organizations that provided access to resources, data, and recent advancements in the field. Their commitment to scientific exploration and education has significantly contributed to the depth and quality of this book.

We also acknowledge the libraries, digital repositories, and journal publishers that have granted access to valuable research articles, clinical studies, and reference materials. Their contributions have been instrumental in compiling evidence-based content that aligns with the latest developments in pharmacology.

Editorial and Publishing Team

Our sincere gratitude goes to the editors, reviewers, and publishing team, whose meticulous efforts have refined this book into its final form. Their expertise in manuscript review, formatting, and quality control has been essential in ensuring clarity, coherence, and readability. Their patience and professionalism in handling revisions, suggestions, and layout enhancements are truly commendable.

Family and Friends

On a personal level, we owe immense gratitude to our families and loved ones, who have provided unwavering support and encouragement throughout this journey. Their patience, understanding, and belief in our work have been a source of motivation, especially during the long hours of research, writing, and revisions.

To our friends and colleagues, who have cheered us on, shared their insights, and provided a listening ear during challenging moments, we are truly grateful for your support. Your encouragement has been invaluable in keeping us focused and driven.

To the Readers

Finally, and most importantly, we dedicate this book to the students, researchers, educators, and healthcare professionals who seek to expand their knowledge and contribute to the ever-growing field of pharmacology. It is our hope that this book serves as a valuable resource, guiding you in your studies, research, and clinical applications.

Pharmacology is a field that continuously evolves, and we recognize that knowledge is a collective effort. We welcome feedback, insights, and discussions from our readers, as they will help shape future editions and contribute to the advancement of this vital discipline.

With heartfelt appreciation,

Mr. Vishesh Kumar Maurya

Ms. Afsha Khan

Dr. Vikas Saxena

Prologue

Today, pharmacology is not merely about understanding how drugs work—it is about optimizing their effects, minimizing adverse reactions, and tailoring treatments to individual patients. The emergence of fields such as pharmacogenomics, nanotechnology, artificial intelligence in drug discovery, and immunopharmacology has opened new frontiers in medicine. No longer are we limited to a "one-size-fits-all" approach; the future of pharmacology is personalized, data-driven, and innovative.

This book serves as a gateway into the world of pharmacology, bridging the gap between fundamental principles and their real-world applications. It explores:

The core principles of drug action, including pharmacokinetics (absorption, distribution, metabolism, and excretion) and pharmacodynamics (drug-receptor interactions and mechanisms of action).

The classification of drugs and their therapeutic applications, covering essential drug categories such as antibiotics, analgesics, cardiovascular drugs, anticancer agents, and central nervous system medications.

The clinical significance of pharmacology, with discussions on drug safety, adverse effects, contraindications, and therapeutic monitoring.

The latest advancements in the field, including biopharmaceuticals, gene therapy, and artificial intelligence-driven drug discovery.

Pharmacology is not just a field of study—it is a lifeline for millions of patients around the world. The development of a single drug requires years of rigorous research, countless clinical trials, and the collaborative efforts of scientists, healthcare professionals, and regulatory agencies. This book acknowledges the dedication of those working tirelessly behind the scenes to bring new treatments to the forefront of medicine.

As we embark on this journey through the science of drugs, let us appreciate the profound impact that pharmacology has on human health. Whether you are a student, educator, researcher, clinician, or an aspiring pharmacologist, this book is designed to guide you through the past, present, and future of drug discovery and therapeutic application.

Let this exploration begin!

CHAPTER ONE

BASICS OF PHARMACOLOGY

Unit-I

Introduction to Pharmacology:-

Pharmacology is the branch of science that studies the effects, mechanisms, and uses of drugs and chemicals on biological systems. It encompasses the understanding of how drugs interact with cellular and molecular processes, the therapeutic and adverse effects of medications, and the principles of drug development and regulation. Pharmacology is divided into various subfields, including pharmacodynamics (how drugs affect the body), pharmacokinetics (how the body absorbs, distributes, metabolizes, and excretes drugs), and clinical pharmacology (the study of drugs in humans). This field plays a crucial role in the development of new therapies and the safe and effective use of medications.

Historical Landmarks in Pharmacology

Ancient and Early Developments

1. **Ancient Civilizations (3000 BCE - 500 CE):**
    - **Egyptians and Mesopotamians:** Utilized plant-based remedies documented in texts like the Ebers Papyrus.
    - **Greeks and Romans:** Hippocrates and Galen made early contributions to the understanding of medicinal substances,

focusing on natural products.

2. **Middle Ages (500 - 1500 CE):**

   - **Avicenna:** His book "The Canon of Medicine" became a reference for medicinal drugs and their properties.
   - **Paracelsus:** Introduced the concept of chemical pharmacology and emphasized the importance of dose in determining a substance's therapeutic or toxic effect.

Renaissance to 19th Century

1. **Renaissance (14th - 17th Century):**

   - **Development of Modern Medicine:** Exploration and colonization led to the discovery of new medicinal plants.
   - **William Withering (1785):** Published his work on the use of foxglove (digitalis) for treating heart conditions, marking a shift toward empirical drug testing.

2. **19th Century:**

   - **Foundation of Modern Pharmacology:** Establishment of pharmacology as a distinct scientific discipline.
   - **Rudolf Buchheim (1847):** Founded the first pharmacology institute in Estonia.
   - **Oswald Schmiedeberg (1870s):** Considered the father of modern pharmacology, his research on drug action mechanisms paved the way for future studies.

20th Century to Present

5. **Early 20th Century:**

- **Paul Ehrlich (1908)**: Developed the concept of the "magic bullet," leading to the development of targeted therapies.
- **Alexander Fleming (1928)**: Discovered penicillin, which revolutionized the treatment of bacterial infections.

6. **Mid to Late 20th Century**:

- **Thalidomide Tragedy (1960s)**: Led to stricter drug regulation and testing protocols.
- **Development of Synthetic Drugs**: Expansion of synthetic chemistry enabled the creation of numerous new drugs.
- **Molecular Pharmacology**: Advances in molecular biology and biochemistry deepened the understanding of drug-receptor interactions.

7. **21st Century**:

- **Pharmacogenomics**: Integration of genetics to tailor drug therapies to individual genetic profiles.
- **Biologics and Biopharmaceuticals**: Development of complex biological drugs, including monoclonal antibodies and gene therapies.
- **Artificial Intelligence and Big Data**: Leveraging computational tools to predict drug interactions and discover new therapeutic compounds.

Scope of Pharmacology
Basic Pharmacology

1. **Pharmacodynamics**:

- **Drug-Receptor Interactions**: Understanding how drugs bind to receptors and elicit biological responses.
- **Mechanisms of Action**: Studying how drugs produce their effects at molecular, cellular, and systemic levels.

2. **Pharmacokinetics:**
   - **Absorption**: How drugs enter the bloodstream.
   - **Distribution**: How drugs are transported throughout the body.
   - **Metabolism**: How drugs are chemically altered, usually in the liver.
   - **Excretion**: How drugs and their metabolites are eliminated from the body.

Applied Pharmacology

3. **Clinical Pharmacology**:
   - **Drug Development and Testing**: From preclinical studies to clinical trials and regulatory approval.
   - **Therapeutics**: Application of drugs to treat diseases, optimize dosages, and manage side effects.
   - **Pharmacovigilance**: Monitoring and evaluating adverse drug reactions to ensure safety.

4. **Toxicology**:
   - **Study of Poisons**: Understanding harmful effects of chemicals and drugs.
   - **Risk Assessment**: Evaluating potential risks associated with exposure to chemicals.

Specialized Fields

5. **Pharmacogenomics**:
   - **Personalized Medicine**: Tailoring drug treatments based on individual genetic profiles to enhance efficacy and reduce adverse effects.

6. **Neuropharmacology**:
   - **Study of Drug Effects on the Nervous System**: Researching treatments for neurological and psychiatric disorders.
7. **Cardiovascular Pharmacology**:
   - **Drugs Affecting the Heart and Blood Vessels**: Developing treatments for heart disease, hypertension, and related conditions.
8. **Biopharmaceuticals**:
   - **Biologics**: Study of complex molecules like proteins, monoclonal antibodies, and gene therapies.
9. **Pharmaceutical Biotechnology**:
   - **Biotechnological Advances**: Leveraging biotech to develop new drug therapies, including vaccines and biosimilars.

Emerging Trends

10. **Nanotechnology**:
    - **Drug Delivery Systems**: Using nanoparticles to improve drug delivery and targeting.
11. **Artificial Intelligence**:
    - **Drug Discovery**: Utilizing AI to predict drug interactions, optimize drug design, and streamline the drug development process.

Nature and Sources of Drugs

Nature of Drugs

1. **Chemical Nature**:

    - **Organic Compounds**: Most drugs are organic compounds, including small molecules and complex biological molecules. Examples include aspirin (a small molecule) and insulin (a biological molecule).
    - **Inorganic Compounds**: Some drugs are inorganic, such as lithium used for bipolar disorder and cisplatin used in cancer treatment.

2. **Physical Nature**:

    - **Solids**: Many drugs are formulated as solid dosage forms like tablets, capsules, and powders.
    - **Liquids**: Some drugs are liquid, such as solutions, suspensions, and emulsions.
    - **Gases**: A few drugs, such as anesthetic gases like nitrous oxide, are administered in gaseous form.

3. **Mechanism of Action**:

    - **Agonists**: Drugs that bind to receptors and mimic the action of endogenous substances.
    - **Antagonists**: Drugs that bind to receptors and block the action of endogenous substances.
    - **Enzyme Inhibitors**: Drugs that inhibit the activity of specific enzymes, such as statins inhibiting HMG-CoA reductase to lower cholesterol.

Sources of Drugs

1. **Natural Sources**:

- **Plants**: Many drugs are derived from plants. Examples include morphine from opium poppy and quinine from cinchona bark.
- **Animals**: Some drugs are obtained from animal sources, such as insulin originally derived from the pancreas of cows and pigs.
- **Microorganisms**: Antibiotics like penicillin are produced by fungi, and other drugs are derived from bacteria and other microorganisms.

2. **Synthetic Sources**:

- **Chemical Synthesis**: Many modern drugs are created through chemical synthesis, allowing for the production of large quantities and the development of novel compounds with specific therapeutic effects.
- **Semi-Synthetic**: Some drugs are partially synthesized from natural products, such as semi-synthetic penicillins which are modified versions of naturally occurring penicillin.

3. **Biotechnology**:

- **Recombinant DNA Technology**: This technology is used to produce complex biological drugs, including monoclonal antibodies and insulin, in microorganisms or cell cultures.
- **Gene Therapy**: Involves the introduction of genetic material into cells to treat or prevent diseases.

Essential Drugs Concept

The concept of essential drugs is a cornerstone of public health and pharmacology, aiming to ensure that the most necessary medicines are available, accessible, and affordable for the entire population. It was pioneered by the World Health Organization (WHO).

Definition

Essential drugs are those that satisfy the priority healthcare needs of the population. They are selected based on their efficacy, safety, cost-effectiveness, and relevance to public health.

Criteria for Selection

1. **Efficacy and Safety**: Drugs must have proven therapeutic benefits and acceptable safety profiles.
2. **Cost-Effectiveness**: The cost of the drug should be justified by its therapeutic benefit and should be affordable to the healthcare system and patients.
3. **Public Health Relevance**: Drugs should address the most significant health problems within a population, including prevalent diseases and conditions.

WHO Model List of Essential Medicines

The WHO publishes a Model List of Essential Medicines, which is updated every two years. This list serves as a guide for countries to develop their own national lists, ensuring that essential medicines are available in sufficient quantities and appropriate forms.

Benefits of the Essential Drugs Concept

1. **Improved Health Outcomes**: Ensures that effective, safe, and affordable medicines are available to treat common diseases and conditions, improving overall health outcomes.
2. **Economic Efficiency**: Focuses resources on the most important medicines, optimizing the use of limited healthcare funds.
3. **Rational Drug Use**: Promotes the appropriate use of medicines, reducing the risk of drug resistance, adverse effects, and wastage.
4. **Equity in Healthcare**: Aims to provide all individuals, regardless of socioeconomic status, with access to necessary medications.

Implementation Strategies

1. **National Essential Medicines Lists**: Countries develop and regularly update their lists based on the WHO model, considering local disease prevalence, healthcare infrastructure, and financial resources.
2. **Policies and Regulation**: Establishing policies to support the procurement, distribution, and rational use of essential medicines.
3. **Education and Training**: Providing healthcare professionals with the knowledge and skills to prescribe and dispense essential medicines appropriately.
4. **Supply Chain Management**: Ensuring efficient procurement, storage, and distribution systems to maintain a consistent supply of essential medicines.

Routes of Drug Administration

1. **Oral (Enteral) Route**:
    - **Description**: Drugs are taken by mouth and absorbed through the gastrointestinal tract.
    - **Advantages**: Convenient, non-invasive, economical, and safe.
    - **Disadvantages**: Variable absorption, possible degradation by stomach acid, first-pass metabolism by the liver.

2. **Parenteral Route**:
    - **Intravenous (IV)**:
        - **Description**: Direct injection into the bloodstream.
        - **Advantages**: Immediate effect, 100% bioavailability, precise control over drug levels.
        - **Disadvantages**: Invasive, risk of infection, higher cost.
    - **Intramuscular (IM)**:

    - **Description**: Injection into a muscle.
    - **Advantages**: Faster absorption than oral, useful for depot formulations.
    - **Disadvantages**: Pain at injection site, limited volume.

  - **Subcutaneous (SC)**:

    - **Description**: Injection into the tissue under the skin.
    - **Advantages**: Slow and sustained release.
    - **Disadvantages**: Limited to small volumes, can cause irritation.

3. **Topical Route**:

   - **Description**: Application to the skin or mucous membranes.
   - **Advantages**: Localized effect, minimal systemic absorption.
   - **Disadvantages**: Limited to surface effects, potential for local irritation.

4. **Transdermal Route**:

   - **Description**: Patches applied to the skin for systemic absorption.
   - **Advantages**: Continuous, controlled release, avoids first-pass metabolism.
   - **Disadvantages**: Possible skin irritation, variable absorption based on skin condition.

5. **Inhalation Route**:

   - **Description**: Drugs are inhaled into the lungs.
   - **Advantages**: Rapid onset, direct effect on respiratory system.
   - **Disadvantages**: Technique-dependent, potential for systemic side effects.

6. **Rectal Route:**
    - **Description:** Drugs are administered via the rectum.
    - **Advantages:** Useful when oral administration is not possible, partially avoids first-pass metabolism.
    - **Disadvantages:** Variable absorption, possible discomfort.
7. **Sublingual/Buccal Route:**
    - **Description:** Drugs are placed under the tongue or between the cheek and gum.
    - **Advantages:** Rapid absorption, avoids first-pass metabolism.
    - **Disadvantages:** Limited to drugs that are effective in small doses.

Agonists and Antagonists

1. **Agonists:**
    - **Description:** Substances that bind to receptors and activate them, mimicking the action of endogenous molecules.
    - **Example:** Morphine is an agonist at opioid receptors, producing analgesia.
2. **Antagonists:**
    - **Description:** Substances that bind to receptors but do not activate them, blocking the action of agonists.
    - **Types:**
        - **Competitive Antagonists:** Compete with agonists for the same binding site on the receptor. Their effect can be overcome by increasing the concentration of the agonist.

        - **Example**: Naloxone is a competitive antagonist at opioid receptors, used to reverse opioid overdose.

    - **Noncompetitive Antagonists**: Bind to a different site on the receptor (allosteric site) or irreversibly to the same site, reducing the maximum effect of the agonist.

        - **Example**: Ketamine is a noncompetitive antagonist at NMDA receptors, used as an anesthetic.

Spare Receptors

- **Description**: A situation where not all available receptors need to be occupied by an agonist to achieve the maximum response. This concept suggests that there are more receptors than are necessary for a full response.
- **Significance**: Allows for a higher sensitivity of the tissue to the agonist, providing a safety margin for receptor functionality.

Addiction, Tolerance, and Dependence

1. **Addiction**:

    - **Description**: A chronic, relapsing disorder characterized by compulsive drug seeking, continued use despite harmful consequences, and long-lasting changes in the brain.
    - **Example**: Opioid addiction.

2. **Tolerance**:

    - **Description**: A decrease in the response to a drug after repeated use, requiring higher doses to achieve the same effect.
    - **Mechanism**: Can result from pharmacokinetic changes (increased metabolism) or pharmacodynamic changes

(receptor desensitization).

3. **Dependence:**
    - **Description:** A state in which the body has adapted to the presence of a drug, leading to withdrawal symptoms when use is reduced or stopped.
    - **Types:**
        - **Physical Dependence:** Manifested by withdrawal symptoms such as tremors, sweating, and nausea.
        - **Psychological Dependence:** Characterized by cravings and emotional need for the drug.

Tachyphylaxis

- **Description:** A rapid decrease in the response to a drug after initial doses, often occurring within a short period.
- **Mechanism:** Often due to receptor desensitization or depletion of mediators.
- **Example:** Nitroglycerin in angina treatment can cause tachyphylaxis, requiring drug-free intervals to restore effectiveness.

Idiosyncrasy

- **Description:** An abnormal, unpredictable reaction to a drug that occurs in a small fraction of individuals, unrelated to the dose.
- **Mechanism:** Often genetic in origin, leading to unusual responses to standard doses of a drug.
- **Example:** Hemolytic anemia in individuals with glucose-6-phosphate dehydrogenase (G6PD) deficiency when exposed to certain drugs like primaquine.

Allergy

- **Description**: An immune-mediated hypersensitivity reaction to a drug, which can range from mild skin rashes to severe anaphylaxis.
- **Mechanism**: Involves the activation of the immune system, often IgE-mediated.
- **Example**: Penicillin allergy, which can cause symptoms from hives to anaphylactic shock.

Pharmacokinetics: An Overview

Pharmacokinetics is the branch of pharmacology that deals with the movement of drugs within the body, encompassing the processes of absorption, distribution, metabolism, and excretion (ADME). Understanding these processes is crucial for optimizing drug therapy, ensuring efficacy, and minimizing toxicity.

Membrane Transport

Drugs must cross cellular membranes to reach their site of action. Membrane transport mechanisms include:

1. **Passive Diffusion**:
    - **Description**: Movement of drugs from an area of high concentration to an area of low concentration without energy expenditure.
    - **Factors**: Lipid solubility, molecular size, and ionization state of the drug.
2. **Facilitated Diffusion**:
    - **Description**: Drug movement across membranes via specific carrier proteins, without energy expenditure.
    - **Characteristics**: Saturable and selective.
3. **Active Transport**:

- **Description**: Movement of drugs against their concentration gradient, requiring energy (usually from ATP).
- **Examples**: P-glycoprotein (P-gp) actively pumps drugs out of cells.

4. **Endocytosis and Exocytosis**:

    - **Description**: Engulfment of drug particles by the cell membrane to form vesicles (endocytosis) or release of substances from vesicles (exocytosis).

Absorption

Absorption is the process by which a drug enters the bloodstream from its site of administration. Factors influencing absorption include:

1. **Route of Administration**: Oral, intravenous, intramuscular, subcutaneous, transdermal, etc.
2. **Formulation**: Tablets, capsules, solutions, etc.
3. **Blood Flow**: Increased blood flow enhances absorption.
4. **Surface Area**: Larger surface areas (e.g., small intestine) enhance absorption.
5. **Drug Solubility**: Lipid-soluble drugs absorb more readily than water-soluble drugs.
6. **pH and pKa**: The ionization state of the drug, influenced by the pH of the environment, affects absorption.

Distribution

Distribution is the process by which a drug is transported from the bloodstream to tissues and organs. Key factors include:

1. **Blood Flow**: Highly perfused organs (e.g., liver, kidney, brain) receive drugs more rapidly.
2. **Plasma Protein Binding**: Drugs bound to plasma proteins (e.g., albumin) are inactive; only free drugs can exert an effect.

3. **Tissue Binding**: Drugs may bind to specific tissues, prolonging their action.
4. **Physiological Barriers**: Barriers such as the blood-brain barrier limit drug distribution to the brain.

Metabolism

Metabolism (biotransformation) is the process by which the body chemically alters drugs. This usually occurs in the liver and involves:

1. **Phase I Reactions (Functionalization)**:
    - **Description**: Introduction or unmasking of functional groups (e.g., hydroxylation, oxidation).
    - **Enzymes**: Primarily cytochrome P450 enzymes (CYP450).
2. **Phase II Reactions (Conjugation)**:
    - **Description**: Conjugation with endogenous substrates (e.g., glucuronidation, sulfation).
    - **Purpose**: Increase water solubility to facilitate excretion.

Excretion

Excretion is the process by which drugs and their metabolites are eliminated from the body. Primary routes include:

1. **Renal Excretion**:
    - **Processes**: Glomerular filtration, tubular secretion, and tubular reabsorption.
    - **Factors**: Kidney function, urine pH, and drug properties.
2. **Biliary Excretion**:

- **Description**: Drugs are excreted into bile and eliminated in feces.
- **Enterohepatic Recirculation**: Drugs can be reabsorbed from the intestine, prolonging their action.

3. **Other Routes**:

- **Lungs**: Volatile anesthetics.
- **Sweat, Saliva, Breast Milk**: Minor routes but important for specific drugs.

Enzyme Induction and Inhibition

1. **Enzyme Induction**:

- **Description**: Increased enzyme activity, usually CYP450, leading to enhanced drug metabolism.
- **Effect**: Reduced drug efficacy due to increased clearance.
- **Examples**: Rifampin and phenobarbital induce CYP450 enzymes.

2. **Enzyme Inhibition**:

- **Description**: Decreased enzyme activity, leading to reduced drug metabolism.
- **Effect**: Increased drug levels and potential toxicity.
- **Examples**: Ketoconazole and grapefruit juice inhibit CYP450 enzymes.

Kinetics of Elimination

1. **First-Order Kinetics**:

- **Description**: The rate of drug elimination is proportional to its concentration.

- **Characteristics**: Constant fraction of drug eliminated per unit time; most drugs follow this kinetics.

2. **Zero-Order Kinetics**:

    - **Description**: The rate of drug elimination is constant and independent of its concentration.
    - **Characteristics**: Constant amount of drug eliminated per unit time; occurs when elimination pathways are saturated.
    - **Examples**: Ethanol and high doses of phenytoin.

Pharmacodynamics: An Overview

Pharmacodynamics is the branch of pharmacology that studies the effects of drugs on biological systems and the mechanisms of their action. It involves understanding how drugs interact with cellular receptors, the relationship between drug concentration and effect, and the body's response to these interactions.

Principles of Drug Action

1. **Drug-Receptor Interaction**:

    - **Binding**: Drugs exert their effects by binding to specific receptors on or within cells. The binding process is often reversible.
    - **Selectivity**: Drugs are designed to be selective for specific receptors to minimize side effects.

2. **Dose-Response Relationship**:

    - **Graded Dose-Response**: The response to a drug is proportional to the dose. It can be represented by a dose-response curve, which shows the relationship between the drug dose and the magnitude of its effect.
    - **Quantal Dose-Response**: Describes the distribution of responses to different doses in a population. It is used to

determine the therapeutic index and safety margin of a drug.

3. **Therapeutic Index (TI):**
    - **Definition:** The ratio between the toxic dose and the therapeutic dose of a drug. A higher TI indicates a greater margin of safety.

Mechanisms of Drug Action

1. **Agonists:**
    - **Description:** Drugs that bind to receptors and activate them, mimicking the effect of endogenous ligands.
    - **Full Agonists:** Produce a maximal response.
    - **Partial Agonists:** Produce a sub-maximal response, even at full receptor occupancy.
2. **Antagonists:**
    - **Description:** Drugs that bind to receptors but do not activate them, blocking the action of endogenous ligands or agonists.
    - **Competitive Antagonists:** Bind reversibly to the same site as the agonist. Their effects can be overcome by increasing the concentration of the agonist.
    - **Non-Competitive Antagonists:** Bind irreversibly or to a different site, reducing the maximal response achievable by the agonist.
3. **Inverse Agonists:**
    - **Description:** Bind to the same receptor as an agonist but induce the opposite pharmacological effect by stabilizing the receptor in its inactive form.

Receptor Theories

1. **Occupancy Theory**:
   - **Description**: The magnitude of a drug's effect is proportional to the number of receptors occupied by the drug. This theory explains the dose-response relationship but does not account for the intrinsic activity of different drugs.
2. **Rate Theory**:
   - **Description**: Suggests that the response to a drug is proportional to the rate of drug-receptor interaction, not just the number of occupied receptors.
3. **Two-State Model**:
   - **Description**: Receptors exist in two states, active and inactive. Agonists stabilize the active state, while antagonists stabilize the inactive state. This model explains the actions of partial agonists and inverse agonists.

Classification of Receptors

Receptors can be classified based on their structure, location, and function:

1. **Ionotropic Receptors**:
   - **Description**: Ligand-gated ion channels that allow ions to pass through the membrane in response to ligand binding.
   - **Example**: Nicotinic acetylcholine receptors.
2. **Metabotropic Receptors**:

- **Description:** G-protein-coupled receptors (GPCRs) that activate intracellular signaling pathways.
- **Example:** β-adrenergic receptors.

3. **Enzyme-Linked Receptors:**

    - **Description:** Receptors with intrinsic enzymatic activity or associated with enzymes upon ligand binding.
    - **Example:** Insulin receptors.

4. **Intracellular Receptors:**

    - **Description:** Receptors located within the cell, typically in the cytoplasm or nucleus, that interact with hydrophobic ligands.
    - **Example:** Steroid hormone receptors.

Regulation of Receptors

1. **Upregulation:**

    - **Description:** Increase in receptor number or sensitivity, often in response to decreased ligand availability.
    - **Mechanism:** Can result from increased synthesis or decreased degradation of receptors.

2. **Downregulation:**

    - **Description:** Decrease in receptor number or sensitivity, often in response to prolonged exposure to high levels of a ligand.
    - **Mechanism:** Can result from receptor internalization, degradation, or desensitization.

3. **Desensitization:**

- **Description**: A temporary reduction in receptor responsiveness after continuous or repeated exposure to a ligand.
- **Types**:
  - **Homologous Desensitization**: Desensitization of a specific receptor due to prolonged exposure to its agonist.
  - **Heterologous Desensitization**: Desensitization of multiple receptor types due to activation of a common signaling pathway.

4. **Receptor Recycling**:
   - **Description**: Internalized receptors are either degraded or recycled back to the cell surface, allowing for restoration of receptor function.

Drug Receptor Interactions and Signal Transduction Mechanisms

Understanding how drugs interact with receptors and the subsequent signal transduction mechanisms is crucial for grasping the pharmacological effects of drugs. Receptors are proteins located on the cell surface or within cells that drugs bind to, initiating a series of intracellular events leading to a biological response.

Types of Receptors and Signal Transduction Mechanisms

1. **G-Protein–Coupled Receptors (GPCRs)**:
   - **Structure**: GPCRs have seven transmembrane domains and are coupled to G-proteins.
   - **Mechanism**: Upon ligand binding, the receptor activates a G-protein by facilitating the exchange of GDP for GTP on the alpha subunit. The activated G-protein then modulates the activity of downstream effectors such as adenylyl cyclase, phospholipase C, or ion channels.

- **Example:** β-adrenergic receptors, which regulate heart rate and bronchodilation.

2. **Ion Channel Receptors:**

    - **Structure:** These receptors are composed of multiple subunits that form a pore through the cell membrane.
    - **Mechanism:** Ligand binding causes a conformational change that opens the ion channel, allowing specific ions (e.g., Na+, K+, Ca2+, Cl-) to flow across the membrane, altering the cell's membrane potential.
    - **Example:** Nicotinic acetylcholine receptors, which mediate synaptic transmission in the nervous system.

3. **Transmembrane Enzyme-Linked Receptors:**

    - **Structure:** These receptors have an extracellular ligand-binding domain, a single transmembrane helix, and an intracellular enzyme domain.
    - **Mechanism:** Ligand binding activates the intrinsic enzymatic activity of the receptor (often a kinase), leading to autophosphorylation and subsequent phosphorylation of downstream signaling molecules.
    - **Example:** Insulin receptors, which regulate glucose uptake.

4. **Transmembrane JAK-STAT Binding Receptors:**

    - **Structure:** These receptors lack intrinsic kinase activity but are associated with Janus kinases (JAKs).
    - **Mechanism:** Ligand binding causes receptor dimerization, activating JAKs, which then phosphorylate the receptor. This creates docking sites for Signal Transducers and Activators of Transcription (STATs). Phosphorylated STATs dimerize and translocate to the nucleus to regulate gene expression.

  - **Example**: Cytokine receptors, which mediate immune responses.

5. **Receptors That Regulate Transcription Factors**:

  - **Structure**: These receptors are typically located in the cytoplasm or nucleus and bind lipid-soluble ligands.
  - **Mechanism**: Ligand binding causes a conformational change, allowing the receptor-ligand complex to bind DNA and regulate the transcription of specific genes.
  - **Example**: Steroid hormone receptors, which regulate gene expression involved in development, metabolism, and immune response.

Dose-Response Relationship

1. **Graded Dose-Response**:

  - **Description**: The relationship between the drug dose and the magnitude of the biological response. It is typically represented by a sigmoidal curve.
  - **Phases**:

    - **Threshold**: Minimum dose required to produce a measurable effect.
    - **Linear Phase**: Response increases proportionally with dose.
    - **Plateau**: Maximum response (E_max) is reached, and further increases in dose do not produce a greater effect.

2. **Quantal Dose-Response**:

  - **Description**: The relationship between the drug dose and the occurrence of a specified response in a population. It is used to determine the effective dose (ED50), toxic dose (TD50), and lethal dose (LD50).

Therapeutic Index (TI)

- **Definition**: The ratio of the toxic dose to the therapeutic dose (TD50/ED50). It provides a measure of a drug's safety margin.
- **Implications**: A high TI indicates a wide safety margin, while a low TI suggests a narrow therapeutic window and a higher risk of toxicity.

Combined Effects of Drugs

1. **Additive Effect**:
    - **Description**: The combined effect of two drugs equals the sum of their individual effects (1 + 1 = 2).
    - **Example**: The combination of two antihypertensive drugs with different mechanisms.
2. **Synergistic Effect**:
    - **Description**: The combined effect of two drugs is greater than the sum of their individual effects (1 + 1 > 2).
    - **Example**: The combination of penicillin and aminoglycosides for bacterial infections.
3. **Antagonistic Effect**:
    - **Description**: One drug reduces or inhibits the effect of another drug (1 + 1 < 2).
    - **Example**: The combination of a β-blocker and a β-agonist.
4. **Potentiation**:

- **Description**: One drug enhances the effect of another drug (0 + 1 > 1).
- **Example**: The combination of caffeine with some analgesics.

Factors Modifying Drug Action

1. **Age**:
    - **Impact**: Pharmacokinetics and pharmacodynamics can vary significantly with age. Pediatric and geriatric patients often require dose adjustments.
2. **Body Weight and Composition**:
    - **Impact**: Dosage may need to be adjusted based on body mass index (BMI) and fat distribution.
3. **Gender**:
    - **Impact**: Hormonal differences and body composition can influence drug metabolism and response.
4. **Genetic Factors**:
    - **Impact**: Genetic polymorphisms can affect drug metabolism, efficacy, and toxicity.
5. **Disease States**:
    - **Impact**: Conditions such as liver or kidney disease can alter drug metabolism and excretion, necessitating dosage adjustments.
6. **Drug Interactions**:

- **Impact**: Concurrent use of multiple drugs can lead to interactions that alter the pharmacokinetics or pharmacodynamics of one or more drugs.

7. **Diet and Lifestyle**:

    - **Impact**: Food, alcohol, and tobacco use can influence drug absorption and metabolism.

Adverse Drug Reactions (ADRs)

Adverse drug reactions (ADRs) are unintended, harmful events associated with the use of medications at normal doses. ADRs can vary in severity and impact patient safety and treatment outcomes.

Types of Adverse Drug Reactions

1. **Type A (Augmented) Reactions**:

    - **Description**: Predictable and dose-dependent reactions related to the pharmacological action of the drug.
    - **Examples**: Hypoglycemia from insulin, bleeding from anticoagulants.

2. **Type B (Bizarre) Reactions**:

    - **Description**: Unpredictable, not dose-dependent, and not related to the pharmacological action of the drug.
    - **Examples**: Anaphylaxis from penicillin, hepatotoxicity from halothane.

3. **Type C (Chronic) Reactions**:

    - **Description**: Associated with long-term therapy and cumulative dose.
    - **Examples**: Adrenal suppression from corticosteroids, tardive dyskinesia from antipsychotics.

4. **Type D (Delayed) Reactions:**
    - **Description:** Delayed effects that may appear after long-term treatment or after discontinuation.
    - **Examples:** Carcinogenesis from chemotherapy, teratogenic effects from thalidomide.
5. **Type E (End-of-Treatment) Reactions:**
    - **Description:** Occur upon withdrawal of the drug.
    - **Examples:** Withdrawal symptoms from opioids, rebound hypertension from clonidine.
6. **Type F (Failure of Therapy) Reactions:**
    - **Description:** Unexpected failure of therapy, often due to drug interactions or resistance.
    - **Examples:** Antimicrobial resistance, contraceptive failure.

Drug Interactions

Drug interactions can occur when the effects of one drug are altered by the presence of another drug, food, or environmental factors. They are classified into pharmacokinetic and pharmacodynamic interactions.

Pharmacokinetic Interactions

Pharmacokinetic interactions involve changes in the absorption, distribution, metabolism, or excretion of a drug:

1. **Absorption:**
    - **Examples:** Antacids can reduce the absorption of certain antibiotics; food can enhance or inhibit drug absorption.
2. **Distribution:**

- **Examples:** Drugs that compete for plasma protein binding sites, such as warfarin and aspirin, can lead to increased free (active) drug levels.

3. **Metabolism:**

    - **Enzyme Induction:** Drugs like rifampin can induce hepatic enzymes, reducing the efficacy of other drugs (e.g., oral contraceptives).
    - **Enzyme Inhibition:** Drugs like ketoconazole can inhibit enzymes, increasing the toxicity risk of other drugs (e.g., statins).

4. **Excretion:**

    - **Examples:** Probenecid inhibits the renal excretion of penicillin, increasing its plasma levels.

Pharmacodynamic Interactions

Pharmacodynamic interactions involve changes in the drug's effect at its site of action:

1. **Additive Effects:**

    - **Example:** Combining two antihypertensive drugs for a greater blood pressure reduction.

2. **Synergistic Effects:**

    - **Example:** The combination of sulfamethoxazole and trimethoprim for a greater antibacterial effect.

3. **Antagonistic Effects:**

- **Example:** Beta-blockers reducing the efficacy of beta-agonists in asthma treatment.

Drug Discovery and Clinical Evaluation of New Drugs

The process of drug discovery and development is complex and involves several phases to ensure the safety and efficacy of new therapeutic agents.

Drug Discovery Phase

1. **Target Identification and Validation:**
   - **Description:** Identifying and validating biological targets (e.g., proteins, genes) involved in disease processes.
2. **Lead Compound Identification:**
   - **Description:** Screening natural products, chemical libraries, or computational models to identify potential lead compounds.
3. **Lead Optimization:**
   - **Description:** Refining lead compounds to improve their pharmacokinetic and pharmacodynamic properties.

Preclinical Evaluation Phase

1. **In Vitro Studies:**
   - **Description:** Laboratory tests on cell cultures to assess biological activity, toxicity, and mechanism of action.
2. **In Vivo Studies:**

- **Description**: Animal studies to evaluate pharmacokinetics, pharmacodynamics, and safety profiles.

3. **Toxicological Testing**:

    - **Description**: Assessing acute, subacute, and chronic toxicity, carcinogenicity, mutagenicity, and reproductive toxicity.

Clinical Trial Phase

Clinical trials are conducted in humans and are divided into four phases:

1. **Phase I**:

    - **Participants**: Small group of healthy volunteers (20-100).
    - **Purpose**: Assess safety, tolerability, pharmacokinetics, and pharmacodynamics.

2. **Phase II**:

    - **Participants**: Larger group of patients with the disease (100-300).
    - **Purpose**: Evaluate efficacy, optimal dosing, and further assess safety.

3. **Phase III**:

    - **Participants**: Large group of patients (1,000-3,000).
    - **Purpose**: Confirm efficacy, monitor side effects, compare with standard treatments, and collect information for drug labeling.

4. **Phase IV** (Post-Marketing Surveillance):

    - **Participants**: General population.

- **Purpose:** Monitor long-term effectiveness, rare adverse effects, and optimal use in various populations.

Pharmacovigilance

Pharmacovigilance involves the detection, assessment, understanding, and prevention of adverse effects or any other drug-related problems.

1. **Adverse Event Reporting Systems:**
   - **Description:** Healthcare professionals and patients report adverse events to regulatory authorities.
2. **Drug Safety Monitoring:**
   - **Description:** Ongoing evaluation of drug safety data from clinical trials, post-marketing surveillance, and literature.
3. **Risk Management Plans:**
   - **Description:** Strategies to minimize risks associated with drug use, including labeling changes, restricted use, or withdrawal from the market.
4. **Regulatory Actions:**
   - **Description:** Regulatory agencies may take actions based on pharmacovigilance data, such as updating warnings, modifying approved uses, or issuing recalls.

Pharmacology of Drugs Acting on the Peripheral Nervous System

The peripheral nervous system (PNS) consists of all the nerves outside the central nervous system (CNS) and includes the autonomic nervous system (ANS) and the somatic nervous system.

This overview focuses on the pharmacology of drugs acting on the PNS, particularly the ANS, which regulates involuntary bodily functions.

Organization and Function of the Autonomic Nervous System (ANS)

The ANS is a critical component of the peripheral nervous system, responsible for regulating involuntary physiological functions, including heart rate, digestion, respiratory rate, pupillary response, urination, and sexual arousal. The ANS is divided into three main divisions:

1. **Sympathetic Nervous System (SNS):**
    - **Function:** Prepares the body for stressful or emergency situations, commonly known as the "fight-or-flight" response.
    - **Neurotransmitters:** Primarily uses norepinephrine (noradrenaline) as the main neurotransmitter, with some functions mediated by acetylcholine.
    - **Receptors:** Adrenergic receptors (alpha and beta receptors).
2. **Parasympathetic Nervous System (PNS):**
    - **Function:** Promotes "rest-and-digest" activities that conserve and restore energy.
    - **Neurotransmitter:** Acetylcholine is the primary neurotransmitter.
    - **Receptors:** Muscarinic and nicotinic receptors.
3. **Enteric Nervous System (ENS):**
    - **Function:** Governs the function of the gastrointestinal system.
    - **Neurotransmitters:** Utilizes a variety of neurotransmitters, including acetylcholine, serotonin, and nitric oxide.

- **Receptors**: Complex interplay of various receptors similar to those in the SNS and PNS.

Drugs Acting on the Autonomic Nervous System

Sympathomimetic (Adrenergic) Drugs

Sympathomimetic drugs mimic the effects of the sympathetic nervous system by activating adrenergic receptors.

1. **Direct-Acting Adrenergic Agonists**:
   - **Examples**: Epinephrine, norepinephrine, dopamine, dobutamine.
   - **Mechanism**: Bind directly to adrenergic receptors (alpha and beta receptors) to stimulate sympathetic activity.
2. **Indirect-Acting Adrenergic Agonists**:
   - **Examples**: Amphetamines, cocaine.
   - **Mechanism**: Increase the release of norepinephrine or inhibit its reuptake, thereby enhancing adrenergic signaling.
3. **Mixed-Acting Adrenergic Agonists**:
   - **Examples**: Ephedrine.
   - **Mechanism**: Combine direct receptor activation with indirect enhancement of neurotransmitter release.

Sympatholytic (Adrenergic Blocking) Drugs

Sympatholytic drugs inhibit the effects of the sympathetic nervous system by blocking adrenergic receptors.

1. **Alpha-Adrenergic Blockers**:
   - **Examples**: Prazosin, phenoxybenzamine.

   - **Mechanism:** Block alpha receptors, leading to vasodilation and decreased blood pressure.

2. **Beta-Adrenergic Blockers:**

   - **Examples:** Propranolol, atenolol, metoprolol.
   - **Mechanism:** Block beta receptors, reducing heart rate, cardiac output, and blood pressure.

Parasympathomimetic (Cholinergic) Drugs

Parasympathomimetic drugs mimic the effects of the parasympathetic nervous system by stimulating cholinergic receptors.

1. **Direct-Acting Cholinergic Agonists:**

   - **Examples:** Pilocarpine, bethanechol.
   - **Mechanism:** Bind directly to muscarinic receptors to stimulate parasympathetic activity.

2. **Indirect-Acting Cholinergic Agonists (Anticholinesterases):**

   - **Examples:** Neostigmine, physostigmine.
   - **Mechanism:** Inhibit acetylcholinesterase, increasing the availability of acetylcholine at synapses.

Parasympatholytic (Anticholinergic) Drugs

Parasympatholytic drugs inhibit the effects of the parasympathetic nervous system by blocking cholinergic receptors.

1. **Muscarinic Antagonists:**

   - **Examples:** Atropine, scopolamine, ipratropium.
   - **Mechanism:** Block muscarinic receptors, reducing parasympathetic activity.

2. **Nicotinic Antagonists:**
    - **Examples:** Mecamylamine (ganglionic blocker), pancuronium (neuromuscular blocker).
    - **Mechanism:** Block nicotinic receptors, affecting both autonomic ganglia and neuromuscular junctions.

Therapeutic Applications

1. **Cardiovascular Disorders:**
    - **Sympathomimetics:** Used in acute heart failure (dobutamine), hypotensive states (norepinephrine).
    - **Beta-blockers:** Used for hypertension, angina, arrhythmias, and heart failure.
2. **Respiratory Disorders:**
    - **Beta2 agonists:** Used for asthma and chronic obstructive pulmonary disease (COPD) (e.g., albuterol, salmeterol).
    - **Anticholinergics:** Used for COPD (e.g., ipratropium).
3. **Gastrointestinal Disorders:**
    - **Cholinergic agonists:** Used for postoperative ileus and urinary retention (e.g., bethanechol).
    - **Anticholinergics:** Used for irritable bowel syndrome and peptic ulcer disease (e.g., dicyclomine).
4. **Ophthalmic Disorders:**
    - **Alpha agonists:** Used for open-angle glaucoma (e.g., apraclonidine).
    - **Muscarinic agonists:** Used for glaucoma (e.g., pilocarpine).

5. **Neurological Disorders:**
   - **Anticholinesterases:** Used for myasthenia gravis (e.g., pyridostigmine).
6. **Anesthesia:**
   - **Neuromuscular blockers:** Used to induce muscle paralysis during surgery (e.g., succinylcholine).

Neurohumoral Transmission

Neurohumoral transmission refers to the process by which nerve cells communicate with each other or with effector organs (muscles, glands) via the release of neurotransmitters. This process involves several steps:

1. **Synthesis:** Neurotransmitters are synthesized in the neuron.
2. **Storage:** Neurotransmitters are stored in synaptic vesicles within the presynaptic neuron.
3. **Release:** Upon receiving an action potential, the neurotransmitters are released into the synaptic cleft.
4. **Receptor Binding:** Neurotransmitters bind to specific receptors on the postsynaptic cell, leading to a physiological response.
5. **Termination:** The signal is terminated by the reuptake of neurotransmitters into the presynaptic neuron, enzymatic degradation, or diffusion away from the synaptic cleft.

Co-transmission

Co-transmission refers to the phenomenon where a single neuron releases multiple types of neurotransmitters or neuromodulators, allowing for more complex and nuanced signaling. This can involve the simultaneous release of classical neurotransmitters (like acetylcholine) and neuropeptides (like substance P), leading to diverse effects on the postsynaptic cell.

Classification of Neurotransmitters

Neurotransmitters can be classified based on their chemical structure:

1. **Amino Acids**:
    - **Examples**: Glutamate (excitatory), Gamma-aminobutyric acid (GABA) (inhibitory), Glycine (inhibitory).
2. **Biogenic Amines**:
    - **Examples**: Dopamine, Norepinephrine, Epinephrine (catecholamines); Serotonin (indolamine); Histamine.
3. **Acetylcholine**:
    - **Function**: Major neurotransmitter in both the central and peripheral nervous systems.
4. **Neuropeptides**:
    - **Examples**: Substance P, Endorphins, Enkephalins, Neuropeptide Y.
5. **Purines**:
    - **Examples**: Adenosine, ATP.
6. **Gases**:
    - **Examples**: Nitric Oxide (NO), Carbon Monoxide (CO).

Parasympathomimetics (Cholinomimetics)

Parasympathomimetics are drugs that mimic the effects of the parasympathetic nervous system by stimulating cholinergic receptors.

1. **Direct-Acting Cholinomimetics:**
    - **Examples:** Pilocarpine, Bethanechol.
    - **Mechanism:** Directly bind to and activate muscarinic receptors.

2. **Indirect-Acting Cholinomimetics (Anticholinesterases):**
    - **Examples:** Neostigmine, Physostigmine.
    - **Mechanism:** Inhibit acetylcholinesterase, increasing acetylcholine levels at synapses.

Parasympatholytics (Anticholinergics)

Parasympatholytics are drugs that inhibit the effects of the parasympathetic nervous system by blocking cholinergic receptors.

1. **Muscarinic Antagonists:**
    - **Examples:** Atropine, Scopolamine, Ipratropium.
    - **Mechanism:** Block muscarinic receptors, reducing parasympathetic activity.

Sympathomimetics

Sympathomimetics are drugs that mimic the effects of the sympathetic nervous system by stimulating adrenergic receptors.

1. **Direct-Acting Adrenergic Agonists:**
    - **Examples:** Epinephrine, Norepinephrine, Dopamine, Dobutamine.
    - **Mechanism:** Directly bind to and activate adrenergic receptors.

2. **Indirect-Acting Adrenergic Agonists:**

- **Examples**: Amphetamines, Cocaine.
- **Mechanism**: Increase the release of norepinephrine or inhibit its reuptake.

3. **Mixed-Acting Adrenergic Agonists**:

- **Examples**: Ephedrine.
- **Mechanism**: Combine direct receptor activation with indirect enhancement of neurotransmitter release.

Sympatholytics (Adrenergic Antagonists)

Sympatholytics are drugs that inhibit the effects of the sympathetic nervous system by blocking adrenergic receptors.

1. **Alpha-Adrenergic Blockers**:

- **Examples**: Prazosin, Phenoxybenzamine.
- **Mechanism**: Block alpha receptors, leading to vasodilation and decreased blood pressure.

2. **Beta-Adrenergic Blockers**:

- **Examples**: Propranolol, Atenolol, Metoprolol.
- **Mechanism**: Block beta receptors, reducing heart rate, cardiac output, and blood pressure.

Neuromuscular Blocking Agents and Skeletal Muscle Relaxants (Peripheral)

Neuromuscular blocking agents and skeletal muscle relaxants are used to induce muscle relaxation during surgical procedures, mechanical ventilation, and other medical interventions.

Neuromuscular Blocking Agents

1. **Non-Depolarizing Neuromuscular Blockers**:

- **Examples**: Pancuronium, Vecuronium, Atracurium.
- **Mechanism**: Compete with acetylcholine for nicotinic receptors at the neuromuscular junction, preventing depolarization and subsequent muscle contraction.
- **Reversal**: Can be reversed by anticholinesterase drugs (e.g., neostigmine).

2. **Depolarizing Neuromuscular Blockers:**

   - **Example**: Succinylcholine.
   - **Mechanism:** Mimic acetylcholine by binding to nicotinic receptors, causing persistent depolarization and subsequent desensitization, leading to muscle paralysis.
   - **Reversal:** Effects are not easily reversed; duration of action is short due to rapid hydrolysis by plasma cholinesterase.

Skeletal Muscle Relaxants (Peripheral)

1. **Centrally Acting Muscle Relaxants:**

   - **Examples**: Baclofen, Diazepam.
   - **Mechanism**: Act on the central nervous system to reduce muscle spasticity by enhancing GABAergic inhibition or other central mechanisms.

2. **Direct-Acting Muscle Relaxants:**

   - **Example**: Dantrolene.
   - **Mechanism:** Inhibits calcium release from the sarcoplasmic reticulum in skeletal muscle, reducing muscle contractions.

Local Anesthetic Agents

Local anesthetics are drugs that cause reversible loss of sensation in a specific area of the body without affecting consciousness. They work by blocking nerve conduction, preventing the propagation of action potentials in nerve fibers. These agents are commonly used for minor surgical procedures, dental work, and pain management.

Mechanism of Action

Local anesthetics block sodium channels in the nerve cell membrane, inhibiting the influx of sodium ions necessary for the generation and propagation of action potentials. This prevents the transmission of nerve impulses, leading to a loss of sensation in the area supplied by the affected nerve.

Classification of Local Anesthetics

Local anesthetics can be classified based on their chemical structure into two main groups:

1. **Esters**:
   - **Examples**: Procaine, Benzocaine, Tetracaine.
   - **Metabolism**: Hydrolyzed by plasma cholinesterases.
   - **Characteristics**: Generally have a shorter duration of action and are more likely to cause allergic reactions due to their ester bond.
2. **Amides**:
   - **Examples**: Lidocaine, Bupivacaine, Mepivacaine.
   - **Metabolism**: Metabolized in the liver by cytochrome P450 enzymes.
   - **Characteristics**: Longer duration of action, less likely to cause allergic reactions compared to esters.

Types of Local Anesthesia

1. **Topical Anesthesia**:
   - Applied directly to the skin or mucous membranes to numb the surface.

   - **Examples**: Lidocaine, Benzocaine.

2. **Infiltration Anesthesia**:

   - Injected into the tissue surrounding a wound or surgical site to block sensory nerve endings.
   - **Examples**: Procaine, Lidocaine.

3. **Nerve Block**:

   - Injection of the anesthetic around a specific nerve or group of nerves to block sensation in a larger area.
   - **Examples**: Bupivacaine, Ropivacaine.

4. **Spinal and Epidural Anesthesia**:

   - Injection into the subarachnoid space (spinal) or epidural space (epidural) to block pain from the lower body.
   - **Examples**: Bupivacaine, Lidocaine.

Side Effects of Local Anesthetics

- **Toxicity**: High plasma concentrations of local anesthetics can lead to central nervous system (CNS) toxicity (e.g., seizures, dizziness) or cardiovascular toxicity (e.g., arrhythmias).
- **Allergic Reactions**: Mostly associated with ester-type local anesthetics, causing symptoms like rash, anaphylaxis.
- **Systemic Absorption**: If injected into vascularized areas, local anesthetics can be absorbed into the bloodstream, leading to systemic effects.

Drugs Used in Myasthenia Gravis

Myasthenia gravis (MG) is an autoimmune disorder characterized by weakness of voluntary muscles, caused by the production of antibodies that block or destroy acetylcholine receptors at the neuromuscular junction. Treatment aims to improve neuromuscular transmission and reduce symptoms.

1. Acetylcholinesterase Inhibitors (Anticholinesterase Agents)

These drugs increase acetylcholine levels at the neuromuscular junction by inhibiting acetylcholinesterase, which normally breaks down acetylcholine.

- **Examples**:
    - **Pyridostigmine**: The most commonly used drug in MG management.
    - **Neostigmine**: Used for short-term management, especially in acute situations.
- **Mechanism**: By inhibiting acetylcholinesterase, these drugs prolong the action of acetylcholine, which helps compensate for the reduced number of acetylcholine receptors.

2. Immunosuppressive Therapy

- **Examples**:
    - **Corticosteroids (e.g., Prednisone)**: Used to suppress the immune response and decrease the production of antibodies against acetylcholine receptors.
    - **Azathioprine**: A cytotoxic drug that suppresses the immune system by inhibiting purine synthesis.
    - **Mycophenolate mofetil**: Another immunosuppressive agent used to decrease autoantibody production.
- **Mechanism**: Immunosuppressive drugs reduce the autoimmune response, thus decreasing the destruction of acetylcholine receptors.

3. Plasmapheresis and Intravenous Immunoglobulin (IVIg)

These therapies are used in severe cases or during exacerbations.

- **Plasmapheresis**: Involves removing the antibodies against acetylcholine receptors from the bloodstream.
- **IVIg**: Provides pooled immunoglobulins that can modulate the immune response.

4. Thymectomy

- **Procedure**: Surgical removal of the thymus gland, which may help in some patients, particularly those with thymomas. It can reduce the severity of symptoms and possibly alter the course of the disease.

Drugs Used in Glaucoma

Glaucoma is a group of eye conditions characterized by increased intraocular pressure (IOP), which can damage the optic nerve and lead to vision loss. The primary goal of treatment is to reduce IOP.

1. Prostaglandin Analogs

- **Examples**: Latanoprost, Bimatoprost, Travoprost.
- **Mechanism**: These drugs increase the outflow of aqueous humor from the eye, thereby lowering IOP. They are often the first-line treatment for open-angle glaucoma.

2. Beta-Blockers

- **Examples**: Timolol, Betaxolol, Carteolol.
- **Mechanism**: Beta-blockers reduce the production of aqueous humor by inhibiting beta-adrenergic receptors in the ciliary body, leading to a decrease in IOP.

3. Alpha Agonists

- **Examples**: Brimonidine, Apraclonidine.
- **Mechanism**: Alpha-agonists decrease aqueous humor production and increase uveoscleral outflow, lowering IOP.

4. Carbonic Anhydrase Inhibitors

- **Examples**: Dorzolamide, Brinzolamide.
- **Mechanism**: These drugs inhibit carbonic anhydrase, an enzyme involved in the production of aqueous humor, leading to decreased secretion of fluid and reduced IOP.

5. Cholinergic Agonists (Miotics)

- **Examples**: Pilocarpine, Carbachol.
- **Mechanism**: These drugs stimulate muscarinic receptors, causing constriction of the pupil (miosis) and improving the outflow of aqueous humor through the trabecular meshwork, thus lowering IOP.

6. Rho Kinase Inhibitors

- **Examples**: Netarsudil.
- **Mechanism**: These agents increase the outflow of aqueous humor through the trabecular meshwork by inhibiting the Rho kinase enzyme, which results in a reduction in IOP.

7. Surgical Treatment

- **Laser Therapy**: Laser trabeculoplasty or laser iridotomy can be used to treat open-angle or angle-closure glaucoma, respectively.
- **Trabeculectomy**: A surgical procedure to create a drainage hole in the eye to reduce IOP.

Pharmacology of drugs acting on central nervous system

Neurohumoral Transmission in the Central Nervous System: Importance of Various Neurotransmitters

Neurohumoral transmission refers to the process by which nerve cells (neurons) in the central nervous system (CNS) communicate with each other through the release and reception of chemical messengers known as neurotransmitters. This process is crucial for regulating physiological processes, maintaining homeostasis, and supporting complex behaviors. Each neurotransmitter has distinct roles and mechanisms of action that contribute to the intricate functioning of the CNS.

1. Overview of Neurohumoral Transmission

The process of neurohumoral transmission begins with the generation of an action potential in the presynaptic neuron. This electrical signal travels down the axon to the synaptic terminal, where it triggers the release of neurotransmitters into the synaptic cleft. These chemical messengers bind to specific receptors on the postsynaptic neuron, resulting in either excitatory or inhibitory effects. The response of the postsynaptic cell depends on the type of neurotransmitter and receptor involved.

Neurotransmitters can be broadly classified as excitatory, inhibitory, or modulatory:

- **Excitatory neurotransmitters** increase the likelihood of generating an action potential in the postsynaptic neuron.
- **Inhibitory neurotransmitters** decrease this likelihood.
- **Modulatory neurotransmitters** regulate the activity of other neurotransmitters and neuronal circuits.

2. Key Neurotransmitters in the CNS

1. Gamma-Aminobutyric Acid (GABA)

GABA is the primary inhibitory neurotransmitter in the CNS. It plays a critical role in maintaining the balance between excitation and inhibition in neuronal circuits. GABA functions by binding to GABA receptors, of which there are two main types:

- **GABA_A receptors**: Ionotropic receptors that increase chloride ion influx, leading to hyperpolarization and inhibition of the postsynaptic neuron.
- **GABA_B receptors**: Metabotropic receptors that modulate potassium and calcium channels via G-proteins, contributing to slower inhibitory effects.

Clinical Significance: Dysregulation of GABAergic signaling is implicated in anxiety disorders, epilepsy, and insomnia. Drugs such as benzodiazepines and barbiturates enhance GABAergic activity.

2. Glutamate

Glutamate is the principal excitatory neurotransmitter in the CNS. It is involved in synaptic plasticity, learning, and memory. Glutamate acts on several receptor types:

- **NMDA receptors**: Ionotropic receptors involved in calcium influx and long-term potentiation.
- **AMPA receptors**: Ionotropic receptors that mediate fast synaptic transmission.
- **Kainate receptors**: Another type of ionotropic receptor with similar excitatory functions.
- **Metabotropic glutamate receptors**: G-protein coupled receptors that modulate synaptic activity.

Clinical Significance: Excessive glutamate activity can lead to excitotoxicity, contributing to neurodegenerative diseases such as Alzheimer's, Huntington's disease, and stroke.

3. Glycine

Glycine serves primarily as an inhibitory neurotransmitter, especially in the spinal cord and brainstem. It binds to glycine receptors, which are chloride ion channels, causing hyperpolarization and inhibition of neuronal activity. Glycine also acts as a co-agonist with glutamate at NMDA receptors.

Clinical Significance: Defective glycine receptor function can cause hyperekplexia, a condition characterized by exaggerated startle responses.

4. Serotonin (5-Hydroxytryptamine, 5-HT)

Serotonin is a modulatory neurotransmitter involved in regulating mood, appetite, sleep, and pain perception. It acts on a broad family of serotonin receptors (5-HT1 to 5-HT7), which include both ionotropic and metabotropic subtypes.

Clinical Significance: Imbalances in serotonin levels are associated with depression, anxiety, and other mood disorders. Selective serotonin reuptake inhibitors (SSRIs) are commonly used to treat these conditions.

5. Dopamine

Dopamine is a modulatory neurotransmitter that influences motor control, motivation, reward, and cognition. It binds to five types of dopamine receptors (D1 to D5), all of which are G-protein coupled receptors.

Clinical Significance: Dopaminergic dysfunction is implicated in Parkinson's disease (reduced dopamine levels) and schizophrenia (abnormal dopamine signaling). Dopamine also plays a central role in the reward pathway and addiction.

General Anesthetics and Pre-Anesthetics: A Comprehensive Overview

General anesthetics are pharmacological agents used to induce a reversible loss of consciousness and sensation, allowing patients to undergo surgical or diagnostic procedures without pain or distress. Pre-anesthetics are medications administered before the primary anesthetic agents to enhance anesthesia, reduce anxiety, and manage physiological responses.

1. General Anesthetics

General anesthetics can be classified into two main categories: inhalational and intravenous agents.

1.1 Inhalational Anesthetics

These agents are administered as gases or vapors and absorbed through the respiratory system.

Common Inhalational Anesthetics:

- **Nitrous Oxide**: Often used in combination with other anesthetics, it provides analgesia and has a rapid onset and recovery.
- **Halothane**: A potent anesthetic with smooth induction but associated with hepatotoxicity.
- **Isoflurane**: Known for its stability and cardiovascular safety.
- **Sevoflurane**: Preferred for pediatric anesthesia due to its pleasant odor and rapid onset.
- **Desflurane**: Characterized by very rapid recovery but requires specialized equipment due to its volatility.

Mechanism of Action: Inhalational anesthetics enhance inhibitory neurotransmission (primarily via GABA receptors) and inhibit excitatory pathways (e.g., NMDA receptors). The exact mechanisms remain partially understood.

Advantages and Disadvantages:

- Advantages: Easy to administer, rapid adjustment of depth of anesthesia.
- Disadvantages: Respiratory depression, potential for postoperative nausea and vomiting (PONV).

1.2 Intravenous Anesthetics

These agents are delivered directly into the bloodstream, providing rapid induction.

Common Intravenous Anesthetics:

- **Propofol**: A widely used agent with rapid onset and short duration of action, known for antiemetic properties.
- **Thiopental Sodium**: A barbiturate with ultra-short-acting properties.
- **Ketamine**: Produces dissociative anesthesia and provides analgesia and amnesia; associated with increased sympathetic

tone.

- **Etomidate**: Known for cardiovascular stability but may cause adrenal suppression.
- **Midazolam**: A benzodiazepine used for induction and conscious sedation.

Mechanism of Action: Most intravenous anesthetics act by potentiating GABA_A receptors or inhibiting NMDA receptors.

Advantages and Disadvantages:

- Advantages: Rapid induction, reduced airway irritation.
- Disadvantages: Cardiovascular and respiratory depression, risk of prolonged sedation with certain agents.

2. Pre-Anesthetics

Pre-anesthetic medications are administered to optimize conditions for general anesthesia and improve patient comfort.

2.1 Categories of Pre-Anesthetics

1. Sedatives and Anxiolytics:

- **Benzodiazepines** (e.g., midazolam, diazepam): Reduce anxiety, provide sedation, and induce amnesia.

2. Analgesics:

- **Opioids** (e.g., morphine, fentanyl): Provide pain relief and reduce the need for higher doses of anesthetic agents.

3. Anticholinergics:

- **Atropine, Glycopyrrolate**: Reduce salivation and bronchial secretions, prevent bradycardia.

4. Antiemetics:

- **Ondansetron**: Prevents postoperative nausea and vomiting.

5. Muscle Relaxants (Adjuncts):

- **Non-depolarizing agents** (e.g., vecuronium) and **depolarizing agents** (e.g., succinylcholine) facilitate intubation and surgical procedures.

6. Gastric Acid Suppressants:

- **H2 receptor blockers** (e.g., ranitidine) and **proton pump inhibitors** (e.g., omeprazole) reduce the risk of aspiration.

Goals of Pre-Anesthetic Medication:

1. Reduce anxiety and provide sedation.
2. Minimize secretions and reflex bradycardia.
3. Provide analgesia and amnesia.
4. Reduce the risk of aspiration and nausea.
5. Facilitate smooth induction and maintenance of anesthesia.

3. Stages of Anesthesia

Anesthesia is traditionally divided into four stages:

1. **Stage 1: Analgesia** – From initial administration until loss of consciousness.
2. **Stage 2: Excitement** – Period of involuntary movements; patient may be agitated.
3. **Stage 3: Surgical Anesthesia** – Characterized by regular respiration and absence of movement.

4. **Stage 4: Medullary Depression** – Respiratory and cardiovascular collapse (avoidance is critical).

4. Monitoring and Safety

During anesthesia, continuous monitoring of vital parameters is crucial:

- **Electrocardiogram (ECG)** for cardiac function.
- **Pulse oximetry** for oxygen saturation.
- **Capnography** for end-tidal carbon dioxide.
- **Blood pressure and temperature** for hemodynamic stability.

Sedatives, Hypnotics, and Centrally Acting Muscle Relaxants: A Detailed Overview

The central nervous system (CNS) is a primary target for a variety of pharmacological agents used to manage anxiety, sleep disorders, and muscle spasticity. Sedatives, hypnotics, and centrally acting muscle relaxants are distinct yet related classes of drugs, each with specific therapeutic uses, mechanisms of action, and clinical considerations.

1. Sedatives

Sedatives, also known as anxiolytics, are drugs that reduce anxiety and exert a calming effect on the CNS without inducing sleep at therapeutic doses. At higher doses, many sedatives can act as hypnotics.

1.1 Common Classes of Sedatives

1. Benzodiazepines

- **Examples**: Diazepam, Lorazepam, Alprazolam.
- **Mechanism of Action**: Enhance the effect of the inhibitory neurotransmitter gamma-aminobutyric acid (GABA) by binding to GABA_A receptors, increasing chloride ion influx and causing neuronal hyperpolarization.

- **Clinical Uses:** Anxiety disorders, acute panic attacks, pre-anesthetic medication.

2. Barbiturates

- **Examples:** Phenobarbital, Pentobarbital.
- **Mechanism of Action:** Prolong the duration of GABA-mediated chloride channel opening.
- **Clinical Uses:** Rarely used for anxiety due to safety concerns, but historically important.

3. Non-Benzodiazepine Sedatives (Z-Drugs)

- **Examples:** Zolpidem, Zaleplon.
- **Mechanism of Action:** Act on benzodiazepine receptors but have a different chemical structure.
- **Clinical Uses:** Short-term treatment of insomnia.

Side Effects: Drowsiness, dizziness, cognitive impairment, potential for dependence and withdrawal.

2. Hypnotics

Hypnotics are agents used to induce sleep. They are typically prescribed for short-term management of insomnia.

2.1 Common Classes of Hypnotics

1. Benzodiazepines

- **Examples:** Temazepam, Triazolam.
- **Clinical Use:** Short-term treatment of insomnia.

2. Non-Benzodiazepine Hypnotics (Z-Drugs)

- **Examples:** Zolpidem, Eszopiclone.
- **Advantages:** Less potential for dependence compared to benzodiazepines.

3. Melatonin Receptor Agonists

- **Example**: Ramelteon.
- **Mechanism of Action**: Agonist at melatonin MT1 and MT2 receptors, regulating sleep-wake cycles.
- **Clinical Use**: Insomnia characterized by difficulty with sleep onset.

4. Antihistamines

- **Examples**: Diphenhydramine.
- **Mechanism of Action**: H1 receptor antagonists.
- **Clinical Use**: Over-the-counter sleep aids.

Side Effects: Daytime sedation, dizziness, risk of dependence with prolonged use.

3. Centrally Acting Muscle Relaxants

Centrally acting muscle relaxants are drugs that reduce muscle tone by acting on the CNS rather than directly on skeletal muscles.

3.1 Common Centrally Acting Muscle Relaxants

1. Baclofen

- **Mechanism of Action**: GABA_B receptor agonist; inhibits excitatory neurotransmission in the spinal cord.
- **Clinical Uses**: Spasticity associated with multiple sclerosis and spinal cord injury.

2. Diazepam

- **Mechanism of Action**: Enhances GABA_A receptor activity.
- **Clinical Uses**: Muscle spasms and spasticity.

3. Tizanidine

- **Mechanism of Action**: Alpha-2 adrenergic agonist; inhibits presynaptic motor neuron activity.
- **Clinical Uses**: Spasticity from neurological conditions.

4. Cyclobenzaprine

- **Mechanism of Action**: Acts on the brainstem to reduce tonic motor activity.
- **Clinical Uses**: Acute muscle spasms.

Side Effects: Sedation, fatigue, dizziness, dry mouth.

4. Differences Between Sedatives, Hypnotics, and Muscle Relaxants

- **Feature**
- **Sedatives**
- **Hypnotics**
- **Muscle Relaxants**
- **Primary Action**
- Reduces anxiety
- Induces sleep
- Reduces muscle spasticity
- **Target**
- CNS
- CNS
- CNS (spinal cord and brainstem)
- **Examples**
- Diazepam, Lorazepam
- Zolpidem, Ramelteon
- Baclofen, Cyclobenzaprine

5. Clinical Considerations and Safety

- **Tolerance and Dependence**: Chronic use of sedatives and hypnotics, especially benzodiazepines, can lead to tolerance, dependence, and withdrawal symptoms.

- **Combination with Alcohol**: Co-administration with alcohol increases the risk of respiratory depression and overdose.
- **Elderly Patients**: More susceptible to sedative effects and cognitive impairment.

Anti-Epileptic Drugs (AEDs): A Detailed Overview

Epilepsy is a neurological disorder characterized by recurrent seizures, resulting from abnormal electrical activity in the brain. Anti-epileptic drugs (AEDs) are pharmacological agents used to control or prevent seizures by modulating neuronal excitability. This document provides a comprehensive analysis of AEDs, their classifications, mechanisms of action, clinical uses, and potential side effects.

1. Classification of Anti-Epileptic Drugs

AEDs are classified based on their primary mechanism of action and specific therapeutic targets:

1.1 Sodium Channel Blockers

These drugs stabilize the inactivated state of voltage-gated sodium channels, reducing neuronal excitability.

- **Examples**: Phenytoin, Carbamazepine, Lamotrigine, Oxcarbazepine.
- **Clinical Uses**: Partial and generalized tonic-clonic seizures.

1.2 Calcium Channel Modulators

These drugs act on voltage-gated calcium channels to reduce neurotransmitter release.

- **Examples**: Ethosuximide (T-type calcium channels), Gabapentin, Pregabalin.
- **Clinical Uses**: Ethosuximide for absence seizures; Gabapentin and Pregabalin for partial seizures and neuropathic pain.

1.3 GABAergic Enhancers

These drugs increase the activity of gamma-aminobutyric acid (GABA), the primary inhibitory neurotransmitter in the CNS.

- **Examples**: Benzodiazepines (e.g., Diazepam, Clonazepam), Phenobarbital, Tiagabine, Vigabatrin.
- **Clinical Uses**: Various seizure types, status epilepticus (benzodiazepines).

1.4 Glutamate Receptor Antagonists

These agents reduce excitatory neurotransmission by antagonizing glutamate receptors.

- **Examples**: Perampanel.
- **Clinical Uses**: Focal seizures.

1.5 Potassium Channel Openers

These drugs increase potassium efflux to hyperpolarize neurons.

- **Example**: Retigabine (Ezogabine).
- **Clinical Use**: Adjunct for partial seizures.

1.6 Synaptic Vesicle Protein 2A Modulators

These drugs bind to synaptic vesicle protein 2A, modulating neurotransmitter release.

- **Example**: Levetiracetam.
- **Clinical Uses**: Broad-spectrum efficacy for focal and generalized seizures.

1.7 Multi-Mechanism Drugs

- **Examples**: Valproate, Topiramate, Zonisamide.
- **Mechanisms**: Affect sodium and calcium channels, enhance GABA activity, and inhibit excitatory neurotransmission.

- **Clinical Uses**: Broad-spectrum use, including absence, myoclonic, and generalized tonic-clonic seizures.

2. Mechanisms of Action of AEDs

AEDs exert their effects through various mechanisms:

1. **Sodium Channel Inhibition**: Reduces repetitive firing of neurons.
2. **Calcium Channel Modulation**: Suppresses abnormal thalamocortical rhythms.
3. **GABA Potentiation**: Enhances inhibitory neurotransmission.
4. **Glutamate Antagonism**: Reduces excitatory activity.
5. **Synaptic Modulation**: Alters neurotransmitter release and synaptic plasticity

Side Effects and Safety Considerations

The side effects of AEDs vary depending on the specific agent and dose:

- **Common Side Effects**: Drowsiness, dizziness, ataxia, fatigue.
- **Serious Side Effects**:
    - **Phenytoin**: Gingival hyperplasia, hirsutism, ataxia.
    - **Carbamazepine**: Agranulocytosis, hyponatremia.
    - **Valproate**: Hepatotoxicity, weight gain, teratogenicity.
    - **Lamotrigine**: Stevens-Johnson syndrome (rash).
    - **Levetiracetam**: Behavioral changes (irritability, aggression).

5. Monitoring and Safety

- **Therapeutic Drug Monitoring**: Important for drugs with a narrow therapeutic index (e.g., phenytoin, carbamazepine).
- **Pregnancy Considerations**: Valproate and certain other AEDs have high teratogenic risk.
- **Drug Interactions**: Many AEDs induce or inhibit cytochrome P450 enzymes, affecting the metabolism of other medications.

6. New and Emerging AEDs

Ongoing research aims to develop drugs with fewer side effects and improved efficacy. Examples include:

- **Brivaracetam**: Similar to levetiracetam but with fewer behavioral side effects.
- **Cannabidiol (CBD)**: Approved for Dravet syndrome and Lennox-Gastaut syndrome.

Alcohols and Disulfiram: A Detailed Overview

Alcohols are a broad class of organic compounds containing one or more hydroxyl (-OH) groups attached to a carbon atom. Ethanol, a widely consumed form of alcohol, is commonly associated with beverages and has significant pharmacological effects. Disulfiram is a drug used in the management of chronic alcoholism by creating an aversive reaction to alcohol consumption. This document explores the chemistry, pharmacology, clinical effects, and therapeutic uses of alcohols and disulfiram.

1. Alcohols

1.1 Ethanol

Ethanol (C_2H_5OH) is the primary alcohol consumed in alcoholic beverages.

Pharmacokinetics:

- **Absorption**: Rapidly absorbed from the stomach and small intestine.
- **Distribution**: Distributes uniformly throughout the body.
- **Metabolism**: Primarily metabolized in the liver by two key enzymes:

  1. **Alcohol Dehydrogenase (ADH)**: Converts ethanol to acetaldehyde.
  2. **Aldehyde Dehydrogenase (ALDH)**: Converts acetaldehyde to acetate.

- **Elimination**: Small amounts are excreted unchanged in urine, sweat, and breath.

Pharmacological Effects:

- **CNS Depression**: Enhances GABAergic activity, inhibits NMDA receptors.
- **Euphoria and Sedation**: Dose-dependent effects ranging from relaxation to stupor.
- **Vasodilation**: Causes flushing and warmth.
- **Diuretic Effect**: Inhibits antidiuretic hormone (ADH).

Chronic Use and Dependence:

- **Tolerance**: Requires increasing amounts for the same effect.
- **Dependence**: Characterized by withdrawal symptoms (tremors, anxiety, seizures).

Adverse Effects:

- **Acute**: Intoxication, impaired judgment, respiratory depression at high doses.
- **Chronic**: Liver disease (fatty liver, hepatitis, cirrhosis), cardiomyopathy, neuropathy.

1.2 Methanol and Isopropanol
Methanol (CH_3 OH):

- **Toxicity**: Metabolized to formaldehyde and formic acid, causing metabolic acidosis and visual disturbances.
- **Treatment**: Ethanol or fomepizole to inhibit alcohol dehydrogenase.

Isopropanol (C_3 H_7OH):

- **Toxic Effects**: CNS depression, respiratory depression, and ketosis without acidosis.

2. Disulfiram

Disulfiram (tetraethylthiuram disulfide) is an aldehyde dehydrogenase inhibitor used to deter alcohol consumption.

2.1 Mechanism of Action

- Inhibits **ALDH**, leading to the accumulation of acetaldehyde when alcohol is consumed.
- Elevated acetaldehyde causes unpleasant effects known as the **disulfiram-ethanol reaction (DER)**.

2.2 Disulfiram-Ethanol Reaction

- **Symptoms**: Flushing, headache, nausea, vomiting, tachycardia, hypotension, chest pain.
- **Severe Reactions**: Arrhythmias, respiratory depression, cardiovascular collapse.

2.3 Pharmacokinetics

- **Absorption**: Well absorbed orally.

- **Duration**: Effects last up to 1-2 weeks after discontinuation due to covalent binding to ALDH.

2.4 Clinical Uses

- **Indication**: Adjunctive therapy for chronic alcoholism.
- **Dosing**: 250-500 mg once daily.

2.5 Adverse Effects

- **Mild**: Drowsiness, metallic taste.
- **Serious**: Hepatotoxicity, polyneuritis, psychotic symptoms.

2.6 Contraindications

- Severe myocardial disease, psychosis, or hypersensitivity to disulfiram.

3. Clinical Considerations and Counseling

- **Patient Education**: Inform patients about the potential severity of the disulfiram-ethanol reaction.
- **Monitoring**: Regular liver function tests.
- **Alcohol Avoidance**: Includes hidden sources like cough syrups and cooking extracts.

Pharmacology of drugs acting on central nervous system

Psychopharmacological Agents: Antipsychotics, Antidepressants, Anti-Anxiety Agents, Anti-Manics, and Hallucinogens

Psychopharmacological agents are medications used to manage various psychiatric and neurological disorders by influencing brain function. This document explores key classes of these agents, their mechanisms of action, clinical uses, and potential side effects.

1. *Antipsychotics*

Antipsychotics are used primarily for the treatment of schizophrenia, bipolar disorder, and psychotic symptoms.

1.1 Typical (First-Generation) Antipsychotics

- **Examples**: Chlorpromazine, Haloperidol.
- **Mechanism**: Dopamine D2 receptor antagonism, reducing positive symptoms of psychosis.
- **Uses**: Schizophrenia, acute psychosis, severe agitation.
- **Side Effects**:
    - Extrapyramidal symptoms (EPS): Dystonia, akathisia, parkinsonism.
    - Tardive dyskinesia with long-term use.
    - Sedation, orthostatic hypotension.

1.2 Atypical (Second-Generation) Antipsychotics

- **Examples**: Risperidone, Olanzapine, Clozapine.
- **Mechanism**: Dopamine and serotonin receptor antagonists.
- **Uses**: Schizophrenia (positive and negative symptoms), bipolar disorder.
- **Side Effects**:
    - Weight gain, metabolic syndrome.
    - Lower risk of EPS compared to typical antipsychotics.
    - Clozapine: Risk of agranulocytosis.

2. *Antidepressants*

These drugs treat depressive disorders by modulating neurotransmitter activity.

2.1 Selective Serotonin Reuptake Inhibitors (SSRIs)

- **Examples**: Fluoxetine, Sertraline.
- **Mechanism**: Inhibit serotonin reuptake, increasing serotonin levels.
- **Uses**: Major depressive disorder, anxiety disorders.
- **Side Effects**: Nausea, sexual dysfunction, insomnia.

2.2 Tricyclic Antidepressants (TCAs)

- **Examples**: Amitriptyline, Imipramine.
- **Mechanism**: Inhibit serotonin and norepinephrine reuptake.
- **Uses**: Depression, chronic pain.
- **Side Effects**: Sedation, anticholinergic effects, cardiotoxicity.

2.3 Monoamine Oxidase Inhibitors (MAOIs)

- **Examples**: Phenelzine, Tranylcypromine.
- **Mechanism**: Inhibit monoamine oxidase enzymes, increasing neurotransmitter availability.
- **Uses**: Atypical depression.
- **Side Effects**: Hypertensive crisis with tyramine-containing foods.

3. Anti-Anxiety Agents

These drugs relieve anxiety symptoms by enhancing inhibitory neurotransmission.

3.1 Benzodiazepines

- **Examples**: Diazepam, Alprazolam.
- **Mechanism**: Enhance GABA-A receptor activity.

- **Uses**: Generalized anxiety disorder, panic attacks.
- **Side Effects**: Sedation, dependence, memory impairment.

3.2 Buspirone

- **Mechanism**: Partial agonist at serotonin receptors.
- **Uses**: Generalized anxiety disorder.
- **Side Effects**: Dizziness, nausea.

4. Anti-Manic Agents

Used in managing bipolar disorder to stabilize mood.

4.1 Lithium

- **Mechanism**: Modulates neurotransmitter release and signaling pathways.
- **Uses**: Bipolar disorder (mania and maintenance).
- **Side Effects**: Tremor, hypothyroidism, nephrotoxicity.

4.2 Valproate

- **Mechanism**: Enhances GABA activity and blocks sodium channels.
- **Uses**: Bipolar disorder, seizure prophylaxis.
- **Side Effects**: Weight gain, hepatotoxicity.

5. Hallucinogens

These substances alter perception, thoughts, and mood.

5.1 Lysergic Acid Diethylamide (LSD)

- **Mechanism**: Serotonin receptor agonist.
- **Effects**: Visual hallucinations, altered consciousness.

- **Risks**: Anxiety, flashbacks.

5.2 Psilocybin

- **Derived From**: Certain mushrooms.
- **Mechanism**: Similar to LSD.
- **Uses**: Experimental in depression and PTSD.

5.3 Phencyclidine (PCP)

- **Mechanism**: NMDA receptor antagonist.
- **Effects**: Dissociation, hallucinations, aggressive behavior.

Agents, Anti-Manics, and Hallucinogens

Psychopharmacological agents are medications used to manage various psychiatric and neurological disorders by influencing brain function. This document explores key classes of these agents, their mechanisms of action, clinical uses, and potential side effects.

1. Antipsychotics

Antipsychotics are used primarily for the treatment of schizophrenia, bipolar disorder, and psychotic symptoms.

1.1 Typical (First-Generation) Antipsychotics

- **Examples**: Chlorpromazine, Haloperidol.
- **Mechanism**: Dopamine D2 receptor antagonism, reducing positive symptoms of psychosis.
- **Uses**: Schizophrenia, acute psychosis, severe agitation.
- **Side Effects**:
  - Extrapyramidal symptoms (EPS): Dystonia, akathisia, parkinsonism.
  - Tardive dyskinesia with long-term use.
  - Sedation, orthostatic hypotension.

1.2 Atypical (Second-Generation) Antipsychotics

- **Examples**: Risperidone, Olanzapine, Clozapine.
- **Mechanism**: Dopamine and serotonin receptor antagonists.
- **Uses**: Schizophrenia (positive and negative symptoms), bipolar disorder.
- **Side Effects**:
    - Weight gain, metabolic syndrome.
    - Lower risk of EPS compared to typical antipsychotics.
    - Clozapine: Risk of agranulocytosis.

2. Antidepressants

These drugs treat depressive disorders by modulating neurotransmitter activity.

2.1 Selective Serotonin Reuptake Inhibitors (SSRIs)

- **Examples**: Fluoxetine, Sertraline.
- **Mechanism**: Inhibit serotonin reuptake, increasing serotonin levels.
- **Uses**: Major depressive disorder, anxiety disorders.
- **Side Effects**: Nausea, sexual dysfunction, insomnia.

2.2 Tricyclic Antidepressants (TCAs)

- **Examples**: Amitriptyline, Imipramine.
- **Mechanism**: Inhibit serotonin and norepinephrine reuptake.
- **Uses**: Depression, chronic pain.
- **Side Effects**: Sedation, anticholinergic effects, cardiotoxicity.

2.3 Monoamine Oxidase Inhibitors (MAOIs)

- **Examples**: Phenelzine, Tranylcypromine.

- **Mechanism**: Inhibit monoamine oxidase enzymes, increasing neurotransmitter availability.
- **Uses**: Atypical depression.
- **Side Effects**: Hypertensive crisis with tyramine-containing foods.

3. Anti-Anxiety Agents

These drugs relieve anxiety symptoms by enhancing inhibitory neurotransmission.

3.1 Benzodiazepines

- **Examples**: Diazepam, Alprazolam.
- **Mechanism**: Enhance GABA-A receptor activity.
- **Uses**: Generalized anxiety disorder, panic attacks.
- **Side Effects**: Sedation, dependence, memory impairment.

3.2 Buspirone

- **Mechanism**: Partial agonist at serotonin receptors.
- **Uses**: Generalized anxiety disorder.
- **Side Effects**: Dizziness, nausea.

4. Anti-Manic Agents

Used in managing bipolar disorder to stabilize mood.

4.1 Lithium

- **Mechanism**: Modulates neurotransmitter release and signaling pathways.
- **Uses**: Bipolar disorder (mania and maintenance).
- **Side Effects**: Tremor, hypothyroidism, nephrotoxicity.

4.2 Valproate

- **Mechanism:** Enhances GABA activity and blocks sodium channels.
- **Uses:** Bipolar disorder, seizure prophylaxis.
- **Side Effects:** Weight gain, hepatotoxicity.

5. Hallucinogens

These substances alter perception, thoughts, and mood.

5.1 Lysergic Acid Diethylamide (LSD)

- **Mechanism:** Serotonin receptor agonist.
- **Effects:** Visual hallucinations, altered consciousness.
- **Risks:** Anxiety, flashbacks.

5.2 Psilocybin

- **Derived From:** Certain mushrooms.
- **Mechanism:** Similar to LSD.
- **Uses:** Experimental in depression and PTSD.

5.3 Phencyclidine (PCP)

- **Mechanism:** NMDA receptor antagonist.
- **Effects:** Dissociation, hallucinations, aggressive behavior.

6. Drugs Used in Parkinson's Disease

Parkinson's disease is characterized by dopaminergic neuron degeneration in the substantia nigra, leading to motor dysfunction.

6.1 Dopaminergic Agents

- **Levodopa (L-Dopa)**:
  - **Mechanism**: Precursor to dopamine that crosses the blood-brain barrier.
  - **Use**: Most effective treatment for motor symptoms.
  - **Side Effects**: Dyskinesia, nausea, on-off phenomenon.
- **Carbidopa**:
  - Combined with levodopa to inhibit peripheral dopa decarboxylase.
  - Reduces nausea and enhances central effects of levodopa.

6.2 Dopamine Agonists

- **Examples**: Pramipexole, Ropinirole.
- **Mechanism**: Directly stimulate dopamine receptors.
- **Uses**: Early-stage Parkinson's, adjunct to levodopa.
- **Side Effects**: Hallucinations, impulse control disorders.

6.3 MAO-B Inhibitors

- **Examples**: Selegiline, Rasagiline.
- **Mechanism**: Inhibit monoamine oxidase B, reducing dopamine breakdown.
- **Uses**: Mild Parkinson's disease.
- **Side Effects**: Insomnia, headache.

6.4 COMT Inhibitors

- **Examples**: Entacapone, Tolcapone.
- **Mechanism**: Inhibit catechol-O-methyltransferase, prolonging levodopa's action.
- **Side Effects**: Diarrhea, liver toxicity (with tolcapone).

6.5 Anticholinergics

- **Examples:** Benztropine, Trihexyphenidyl.
- **Mechanism:** Block muscarinic receptors, reducing tremors.
- **Side Effects:** Dry mouth, blurred vision.

7. Drugs Used in Alzheimer's Disease:

Alzheimer's disease (AD), a progressive neurodegenerative disorder affecting millions worldwide, has no definitive cure. However, several drugs aim to alleviate symptoms and slow disease progression. Let's explore the key categories of medications currently approved for managing Alzheimer's:

1. Cholinesterase Inhibitors

These drugs boost the levels of acetylcholine, a neurotransmitter critical for memory and learning, which decreases in Alzheimer's patients.

- **Examples:**
    - **Donepezil (Aricept):** Used for mild, moderate, and severe Alzheimer's.
    - **Rivastigmine (Exelon):** Available as a capsule or transdermal patch.
    - **Galantamine (Razadyne):** Prescribed for mild to moderate AD.
- **Benefits:** May improve cognitive symptoms and delay functional decline.
- **Side Effects:** Nausea, vomiting, and diarrhea are common.

2. NMDA Receptor Antagonists

These drugs regulate the activity of glutamate, a chemical involved in memory and learning, by preventing overstimulation that can damage neurons.

- **Example:**
    - **Memantine (Namenda):** Approved for moderate to severe Alzheimer's.
- **Benefits:** Helps with memory, attention, and performing daily tasks.
- **Side Effects:** Dizziness, headache, and confusion.

3. Combination Therapy

Combining cholinesterase inhibitors and NMDA receptor antagonists offers a broader approach to symptom management.

- **Example:**
    - **Donepezil and Memantine (Namzaric):** Used for moderate to severe cases.

4. Emerging Treatments

- **Aducanumab (Aduhelm):** A monoclonal antibody targeting amyloid-beta plaques. Although controversial, it was approved by the FDA in 2021 under accelerated approval.
- **Lecanemab (Leqembi):** Another monoclonal antibody that has shown promise in early Alzheimer's stages.

CNS Stimulants and Nootropics:

In today's fast-paced world, enhancing mental performance is a growing priority for many. Two common categories of substances linked to cognitive enhancement are **Central Nervous System (CNS) Stimulants** and **Nootropics**. Here's a closer look at their mechanisms, uses, and potential risks:

1. CNS Stimulants

CNS stimulants increase the activity of brain chemicals like dopamine and norepinephrine, enhancing alertness, attention, and energy levels.

- **Common CNS Stimulants**:
    - **Caffeine**: Found in coffee, tea, and energy drinks, caffeine improves wakefulness and concentration.
    - **Amphetamines (Adderall)**: Prescribed for ADHD and narcolepsy to boost focus and impulse control.
    - **Methylphenidate (Ritalin)**: Another ADHD medication that helps with attention and hyperactivity.
- **Benefits**:
    - Improved focus and productivity.
    - Treatment of medical conditions like ADHD and sleep disorders.
- **Risks and Side Effects**:
    - Insomnia, increased heart rate, and anxiety.
    - Potential for abuse and addiction, especially with prescription stimulants.

2. Nootropics

Nootropics, often called "smart drugs" or cognitive enhancers, are substances that may improve brain function without the stimulant effects. They can be natural or synthetic.

- **Examples of Nootropics**:
    - **Piracetam**: One of the earliest synthetic nootropics used for memory enhancement.

- **L-theanine**: Found in green tea, it promotes relaxation and focus.
- **Bacopa Monnieri**: An herbal supplement believed to enhance memory and reduce anxiety.
- **Modafinil**: A prescription medication for narcolepsy, often used off-label for cognitive boosting.

- **Benefits**:
  - Enhanced memory, creativity, and motivation.
  - Neuroprotective effects in some cases.

- **Risks and Considerations**:
  - Long-term safety is unclear for many nootropics.
  - Side effects may include headaches, gastrointestinal issues, or mood swings.
  - Over-reliance can lead to dependency on perceived cognitive benefits.

Opioid Analgesics and Antagonists: A Comprehensive Overview

Opioids play a crucial role in pain management, yet their use comes with significant risks and challenges. Understanding opioid analgesics and their antagonists is essential for effective and responsible clinical practice.

Opioid Analgesics

Opioid analgesics, also known as narcotic pain relievers, are medications used to treat moderate to severe pain. They work by binding to specific opioid receptors in the brain, spinal cord, and other areas of the body to reduce pain perception.

Mechanism of Action

Opioid receptors are classified into three major types:

- **Mu (μ) receptors**: Responsible for analgesia, euphoria, respiratory depression, and physical dependence.
- **Delta (δ) receptors**: Contribute to analgesia and modulation of mood.
- **Kappa (κ) receptors**: Associated with pain relief, sedation, and dysphoria.

When opioid agonists bind to these receptors, they mimic the effects of endogenous opioids, providing pain relief.

Common Opioid Analgesics

1. **Morphine**: The standard opioid for severe pain management.
2. **Codeine**: Often used for mild to moderate pain and cough suppression.
3. **Oxycodone (OxyContin)**: Prescribed for moderate to severe chronic pain.
4. **Hydrocodone (Vicodin)**: A combination opioid often paired with acetaminophen.
5. **Fentanyl**: A synthetic opioid 50-100 times more potent than morphine, used in acute and chronic pain, particularly for cancer patients.
6. **Methadone**: Used for chronic pain and in medication-assisted treatment for opioid dependence.

Benefits of Opioid Analgesics

- **Effective Pain Relief**: Critical for managing postoperative pain, cancer-related pain, and acute injuries.
- **Improved Quality of Life**: When used appropriately, opioids can significantly enhance comfort and mobility.

Risks and Adverse Effects

- **Tolerance**: Reduced effectiveness over time, requiring higher doses.

- **Dependence and Addiction**: High potential for misuse and addiction.
- **Respiratory Depression**: A life-threatening side effect in overdose situations.
- **Other Side Effects**: Nausea, constipation, sedation, and itching.

Opioid Antagonists

Opioid antagonists are medications that block the effects of opioids by binding to opioid receptors without activating them. They are crucial in treating opioid overdoses and reversing opioid-induced respiratory depression.

Common Opioid Antagonists

1. **Naloxone (Narcan)**
   - **Mechanism**: Binds to mu, kappa, and delta receptors, reversing opioid effects within minutes.
   - **Uses**: Emergency treatment of opioid overdoses. Available as nasal sprays and injectables.
2. **Naltrexone**
   - **Mechanism**: Long-acting opioid receptor antagonist.
   - **Uses**: Used in addiction treatment to prevent relapse by blocking euphoric effects.
3. **Methylnaltrexone**
   - **Mechanism**: Peripherally acting mu-opioid receptor antagonist.
   - **Uses**: Treats opioid-induced constipation without affecting central pain relief.

Benefits of Opioid Antagonists

- **Life-saving in Overdose**: Naloxone has dramatically reduced opioid-related fatalities.
- **Support for Addiction Treatment**: Naltrexone supports long-term recovery by reducing cravings and blocking reinforcement.

Challenges and Considerations

- **Timing and Access**: Rapid administration of naloxone is critical during overdoses.
- **Withdrawal Symptoms**: Sudden opioid reversal can cause severe withdrawal symptoms in dependent individuals.

Drug Addiction, Drug Abuse, Tolerance, and Dependence:

Substance use and its related consequences remain significant public health issues worldwide. Understanding the concepts of **drug addiction, drug abuse, tolerance**, and **dependence** helps to clarify the nature of substance use disorders and informs strategies for prevention and treatment.

1. Drug Addiction

Drug addiction, also known as substance use disorder (SUD), is a chronic, relapsing brain disorder characterized by the compulsive use of drugs despite harmful consequences. It is driven by changes in the brain's reward system and decision-making processes.

Key Features

- **Craving**: A strong desire or urge to use the substance.
- **Loss of Control**: Difficulty in cutting down or controlling drug use.
- **Continued Use Despite Harm**: Persisting in using the substance even when it causes personal, social, or health problems.

Neurobiological Mechanisms

- Drugs stimulate the release of dopamine in the brain's **reward circuit**, reinforcing pleasurable feelings. Over time, the brain adapts, requiring more of the drug to achieve the same effect.

Examples of Addictive Substances

- **Alcohol**
- **Opioids (e.g., heroin, prescription painkillers)**
- **Stimulants (e.g., cocaine, methamphetamine)**
- **Nicotine**

Symptoms of Addiction

- Obsession with obtaining and using the substance.
- Neglect of responsibilities and relationships.
- Physical and psychological withdrawal symptoms when not using the substance.

2. Drug Abuse

Drug abuse refers to the improper or harmful use of drugs for non-medical purposes or in a manner that deviates from prescribed guidelines.

Examples of Drug Abuse

- Taking higher doses of prescription medications than prescribed.
- Using recreational drugs like cocaine or ecstasy.
- Misusing over-the-counter medications such as cough syrups containing codeine.

Consequences of Drug Abuse

- **Health Effects:** Liver damage, cardiovascular problems, mental health disorders.
- **Social Effects:** Strained relationships, poor academic or job performance.

- **Legal Issues**: Arrests for possession or driving under the influence.

3. Tolerance

Tolerance occurs when a person's response to a drug diminishes over time, requiring higher doses to achieve the same effect.

Mechanism

- Repeated exposure to a drug leads to **neuroadaptation**, where the brain adjusts to the presence of the drug, reducing its effectiveness.

Types of Tolerance

- **Pharmacodynamic Tolerance**: Changes in receptor sensitivity or number.
- **Metabolic Tolerance**: Increased metabolism of the drug, reducing its blood concentration.

Examples

- A person with chronic pain requiring increased doses of opioids for pain relief.
- Increased caffeine consumption to achieve the same level of alertness.

Risks

- Increased tolerance can lead to higher dosages and escalate the risk of overdose.

4. Dependence

Dependence refers to a physical or psychological need for a drug to function normally. It can develop with repeated use of certain substances, including both addictive and non-addictive drugs.

Types of Dependence

- **Physical Dependence**: Characterized by withdrawal symptoms when the drug is stopped.
    - **Examples of Withdrawal Symptoms:**
        - Opioids: Nausea, muscle aches, insomnia.
        - Alcohol: Tremors, seizures, hallucinations.
- **Psychological Dependence**: Emotional or mental reliance on a substance to relieve stress or feel pleasure.

Examples

- Chronic benzodiazepine users experiencing severe anxiety when stopping medication.
- Long-term nicotine users struggling with cravings and irritability upon cessation.

Relationship Between Tolerance, Dependence, and Addiction

- **Tolerance** often precedes **dependence**, but not all cases of tolerance lead to addiction.
- **Dependence** can occur without addiction, as seen in patients taking opioids for chronic pain under medical supervision.
- **Addiction** includes psychological elements such as cravings and compulsive behavior, beyond the physical need for the drug.

www.ingramcontent.com/pod-product-compliance
Lightning Source LLC
LaVergne TN
LVHW091118150826
845673LV00002B/889

* 9 7 9 8 8 9 7 2 4 0 9 7 5 *